"Mary's story is one that will live deep in the corners of your heart forever, reminding you, through her own experiences and beautiful storytelling, that the good stuff of life is often found in the hardest circumstances. *Dirt* is the inspiring story of a girl who knew something better was on the other side of fear and challenge. Mary's words are so poignant and touched my heart in so many ways. This is a story you will keep with you long after you turn the final page. I'm so excited to share this truly extraordinary memoir with everyone I know, and I'm eager for Mary to put pen to paper again."

Emily Ley, bestselling author of *When Less Becomes More: Making Space for Slow, Simple, and Good*

"Mary Marantz is a born storyteller! She is an exceptional writer who has that unique ability to transform even the hardest of scenes into profound fine art. Her writing just has a way of taking you by the hand and walking you back to truth, to a place called home. If you're tired of running from your story and ready to lean into the strength it gives you, this book is for you. *Dirt* is truly a pull-yourself-up-by-the-bootstraps American anthem. All I could think was how our two stories are so different, and yet Mary's story is also my own. It's all of our stories. This deeply moving debut book is a triumph in every way!"

Jessica Honegger, founder of Noonday Collection and author of *Imperfect Courage*

"In Philippians, the apostle Paul talks about the great stuff he's done, the horrible stuff he's been through, and how it's all forgettable in light of God. Those verses come to mind when I hear or read Mary's words. Her story matters because all of our stories matter—but it's not her accolades or her acknowledgments of pain that you'll remember most. Her words reek of God's grace, glory, and goodness, and of our ability to cling to them. Whether you come to this book with the most successful or the most stinky past, you'll be blessed and loved well by Mary's leading. She's a good friend, and this is a good book."

Jess Connolly, author of *You Are the Girl for the Job* and *Take It Too Far*

"In this captivating, compelling book, Mary Marantz draws you into a moving story with plenty of space to breathe and say, 'I've felt that too.' Marantz writes from right here on the ground, meeting you where you are. She tells the unique story of her life in a beautifully relatable way, where you will comb through every page and be reminded: through it all, there is grace."

Morgan Harper Nichols, author of *All Along You Were Blooming: Thoughts for Boundless Living*

"It's easy to want to discard your roots and turn away from the mess that made you, but Mary Marantz does just the opposite in this beautiful work. Filled with the kind of writing that drops you directly into the gritty details of the story, Mary sifts through her own 'dirt' to reveal pure treasures and glimpses of God to hold on to for the long haul. This book is gorgeously written, and every last word is so intentionally placed. The words are stunning. The pictures she paints are so real, I could not put it down! Get ready to have your heart shaken up and made better through the pages of this book."

Hannah Brencher, author of *Come Matter Here* and *Fighting Forward* (2021)

"How is it possible to find myself within a story that is so different from my own? Through gorgeous writing and brave truth telling, Mary guides us to lean into our own stories and find transformation and redemption we never thought possible. *Dirt* is an anthem of love over circumstances and faith over fear. I dare you to start this book and not read it in one sitting. I know it will leave you inspired, challenged, and changed."

Nicole Zasowski, marriage and family therapist and author of *From Lost to Found*

"*Dirt* is a beautifully written memoir that I could barely put down. Mary's words are equal parts poetry and pain, sadness and soaring redemption. For every one of us who has ever wished for an easier story, *Dirt* is the fight song we have been waiting for. An invitation to trade shame, striving, perfectionism, and unforgiveness for grace, rest, freedom, and reconciliation. I found myself repeatedly nodding my head, seeing myself in her story, even though our pasts could not be more different. I can't think of a more important, desperately needed message right now. This book is a wakeup call, a resounding reminder to stop running and to dig deep into the mud that made us."

Tonya Dalton, bestselling author of *The Joy of Missing Out*

"One word: riveting. If you're looking for your next page-turner that will make you believe anything is possible for yourself, *Dirt* is what you need to read."

Jess Ekstrom, author of *Chasing the Bright Side*

dirt

dirt

growing strong roots
in what makes
the broken beautiful

MARY MARANTZ

a division of Baker Publishing Group
Grand Rapids, Michigan

© 2020 by Mary Marantz

Published by Revell
a division of Baker Publishing Group
PO Box 6287, Grand Rapids, MI 49516-6287
www.revellbooks.com

Printed in the United States of America

Library of Congress Cataloging-in-Publication Data
Names: Marantz, Mary, author.
Title: Dirt : growing strong roots in what makes the broken beautiful / by Mary Marantz.
Description: Grand Rapids, Michigan : Revell, a division of Baker Publishing Group, 2020.
Identifiers: LCCN 2020014600 | ISBN 9780800738457 (cloth)
Subjects: LCSH: Marantz, Mary—Family. | Women—West Virginia—Nicholas County—Biography. | Fathers and daughters—West Virginia—Biography. | Nicholas County (W. Va.)—Social life and customs. | Yale Law School—Students—Biography. | Nicholas County (W. Va.)—Biography. | Imperfection. | Christian biography.
Classification: LCC CT275.M4574 A3 2020 | DDC 975.4/69092 [B]—dc23
LC record available at https://lccn.loc.gov/2020014600

Scripture quotations are from The Holy Bible, English Standard Version® (ESV®), copyright © 2001 by Crossway, a publishing ministry of Good News Publishers. Used by permission. All rights reserved. ESV Text Edition: 2016

Photo on page 55 courtesy of the Library of Congress Prints and Photographs Division, LC-DIG-fsa-8a39820.

Published in association with Illuminate Literary Agency, www.Illuminateliterary.com.

Some names and details have been changed to protect the privacy of the individuals involved.

Interior design by William Overbeeke.

20   21   22   23   24   25   26   7   6   5   4   3   2   1

For Dad, Mom, and Goldie,
who loved the Girl In the Trailer.
For Justin,
who loved the Girl After the Trailer.
I have been born a new thing.
This time, one with both roots and wings.

For the people of West Virginia,
who are unshakable proof of the indomitable spirit
that grows wild in the mountains there.

This story belongs to all of us.

PART II: the girl after the trailer

prologue

HIS HANDS LOOKED even dirtier than I'd remembered, resting against the crisp, white, sterile sheets of a bed tucked away in the far-flung outer reaches of the hospital corner.

I was standing in the same hospital I'd been born in some thirty-six years earlier in the spring of 1980, when Mom was already a wife of three years just two months shy of her twenty-first birthday, and he had yet to find his way to wanting to be a father. But from the first time he held me, I had been my father's child, and that had been both our unraveling and the common thread that stitched us back together again.

Once, we had known what it was to roar at one another—to shout and spit and fight and rail against one another with all the similarities in us that drove us to our differences. With all the stubbornness and set-in-our-ways that made us both so very much the same. We once knew what it was to fight with one another—and *for* one another. To hold on with a white-knuckle grip when everything and everyone around us was letting go. And now the *blip-blip-blip* of the machines casting their pale green light on everything standing between us—my leaving, my running, my staying gone—was the loudest noise in the room.

It had been five years since I had been back home. Not since we laid Goldie in the cold September ground, when Dad and I sat under a cheap tent awning covering her newly open wound of a grave long after everyone else had gone. We held on to each other and cried stinging, biting tears as the rain picked up all around us and thrummed out a holy, haunting rhythm turned hymn on the vinyl above.

A few hours before the tent, I had stood in a small, red-velvet-clad funeral home and delivered the eulogy for my beloved grandmother to a room only half full of people, a few of which might have preferred it if I'd just stayed gone. I hadn't been bothered to be there when she died, so why should I be the one to get the final word? A day later, Dad moved from our old brown single-wide trailer into Goldie's little red, suddenly empty house next door—the same house where he had both grown up and grown up way too fast—while my mom went back to her motel.

A year later, he was vomiting up blood every day. It would come upon him with such a suddenness and violence that it didn't so much spill out of him as erupt from his lips. He rarely made it to the bathroom in time, and as such, Goldie's pristine green carpeting—the same she had chosen fifteen years prior because it perfectly matched her pretty pink-and-green flowered couch—was now streaked in deep shades of dark, dried crimson. Battle stripes that perfectly matched the starry dots of the same kind splattered on the ceiling above. Had she not already been dead, the sight of it surely would have killed her.

I could just picture her now, up there on the top of Holcomb Holler, where our family cemetery rested in a small field surrounded by a sentinel of overgrown weeds. Where I like to imagine that the ghosts of our ancestors herald you up the twisting, turning knots of dirt road, rushing and whispering beside a motorcade of black cars as they make their unhurried, mournful crawl up the mountainside, ushering the next body on to its resting place with a refrain as low and lonesome as the slow pull of rosin on strings. Kindred souls just walking each other home. There, in my mind, Goldie would be doing exactly what she always said she'd do if any of us ever did something to disappoint her: spinning in her grave and cussing like a sailor under her dissipated breath, despite the good church lady she'd always been.

Being my father, a man known far and wide for such bumper-sticker faith as "I'm tough, I can take it" and "Ohhh, it'll be alright," it had taken him far too long to go to the doctor. Now his insides were eaten up with the cancer, three tumors that had grown into one. He had lost sixty pounds through the ordeal. And it had mined and hollowed out his face in such a way—aged him twenty years seemingly overnight—that I could hardly recognize him now. My breath caught in my throat when I walked into the dim light of that hospital room and saw him, a man much older than I had left him. I had to look away so he wouldn't see the horror in my eyes. And I was left staring at his dirty hands leaving marks on the crisp, white sheets.

They were the only thing left about him that I recognized.

From the hallway, I could hear the nurses at their station—their accents sounded both foreign and familiar at the same time, like the two different versions of myself that I now held inside me couldn't agree on which one it was. There was the me who was the Girl In the Trailer . . . and then there was the me who came after. And they had both come to stand by my father's bedside, knowing full well they should have come much sooner.

It had been five years since I had been home to Nicholas County, West Virginia, but I hadn't lived there in eighteen. And at that moment I was, in every way, both a girl and a woman divided: eighteen years at home and eighteen years since I'd left. I had just crossed some unspoken threshold of a finish line where I'd now spent as much of my life outside of that trailer as I had in it. And thinking back on it right then, it felt much less like a memory and more like another lifetime.

In the flickering, green, beeping darkness, Dad's eyes rolled forward—slow, wincing, as if that effort alone might finish him—blinked, and then opened.

"Hey, Kid. How we doing?"

It had been years since he'd called me Kid. Not since I left for law school at Yale and he finally, for the first time in my life, started calling me Mary. He'd visited me exactly twice in New Haven in the three years I was in school there—once to help me find an apartment and once to move me in. Neither visit was to come back and watch me walk across the stage when I graduated. A lifetime of work to help get me to that place, and he wasn't even there to witness it. But I had at least graduated to my given name, and that felt like something. So to hear him call me Kid now, in the small, still darkness of this unfamiliar room, it felt like he wasn't so much in another place as another time.

My first thought was that they must have him on some powerful pain medicine, and that through an IV-induced fog he was just pretty out of it. I traced the tube coming out of his arm to a clear bag of liquid hanging from a metal stand and churning out its *drip, drip, drip* rhythm till all the drips and blips in the room seemed to be keeping time with one another, and I felt like I might lose my mind at the repetition and replaying of it all. It was like scenes from a projector reel were casting mere shadows of our life—both he and I together, and he and I apart—on the sanitized, whitewashed walls all around us. They blurred and bled into one another in a way that began to rewind time, my past, present, and future all melting into one. And I couldn't bring myself to look at anything but the hands that helped build me.

"Kid, Kid, Kidster. I was praying that you'd come."

Now I was certain. The time to be worried was here.

The only church on Sunday where JR Bess had ever worshiped was at the altar of the woods. His congregation was a canopy of trees ripe for the cutting. His preacher was a busted-up, run-down John Deere 550 dozer always pushing him, driving him on toward his higher power. To me, he was not a man who ever seemed to be on real good terms with God. And to take one look at the struggle that was his life, it would be easy to assume that God had been more than fine with that arrangement. As far as I knew, Dad hadn't prayed for anything or *anyone* a day in his life.

And I had no idea why he'd be starting now.

PART I

the girl
in the
trailer

it always started with dirt

FROM THE EDGE of a dirt path off of Airport Road, where the road forks and snakes just a little taller to form the highest point on Fenwick Mountain, you can stand and watch a storm roll in from any and all directions.

We would do that often when I was little. We'd stand out under the wooden overhang of a hand-built lean-to turned front porch—where the boards were all mismatched scraps of whatever you could find and the nails, half-hammered and crooked, sat rusted from the punishment of a blistering summer sun—and watch as streaks of lightning lit up the heat of a July night sky. While thunder rumbled hard and shook the mountains.

Dad stood next to me in his muddy jeans and a long-since-yellowed white undershirt, his bare, battered feet on the dirt floor of the porch. His dark hair wild, as if standing on end at the electricity of it all.

"Sure is pretty, ain't it, Kid? Y'know, if you listen close and count, you can tell how far away it is."

The next lightning flashed, and we started counting together. We only got to two-Mississippi before we heard that low rumble of thunder rising up again. This storm wasn't coming. It was already on top of us.

When the rain came, it washed over us in sheets and waves, hammering out a Johnny Cash train-track *get-a-rhythm* on the tin-can roof of our single-wide trailer that paired nicely with the lonesome whistle-will of the wind through the chimes Mom had hung just outside my window. A true West Virginia lullaby if ever I heard one.

That night, as we stood and stared into the face of the storm—the kind of earth-shaking furor that makes you feel like the hand of God itself is hovering just a few feet above the ground with a finger pointed directly at you—we froze as lightning met ground just two houses down, and their transformer lit up and started sparking like a Roman candle. The house was spared, but the garage burned down and with it the family dog. Well, technically he died when the fire department answering the call had to shoot him to put him out of his misery, but he was lost nonetheless.

The mountain I come from was never easy on animals.

I was not a beautiful child.

Gap-toothed, with a mess of wild, curly brown hair—the chemically altered kind so synonymous with the eighties and that decade's particular love of cheap home perms, big hairspray bangs, and the chance to change whatever lot in life you'd naturally been given. I had eyes that were set too close together, lips that were far too thin, and—to add insult to injury—my father's nose set right in the middle to remind all the other features that they were playing far too small.

In the summer of 1989, you would have found me bare-legged and slightly bloody from the latest round of briar-patch scratches, shouting out an answer over my shoulder at the request to be back by dark while lighting out as fast as my gangly, all-too-tall-for-my-age limbs would carry me across the overgrown field behind our trailer. I was forever making my way into the deep, dark woods that lay just beyond the weeds . . . beckoned ever onward by their siren call.

In the shelter and shadow of the woods, I could be whoever I wanted.

There are a lot of things I'm going to tell you about how I grew up, but before we get there, I need you to know something: this part—*the part with the woods*—well, I wouldn't change that at all.

From birth until I left at eighteen, I grew up on the very top of a mountain in rural West Virginia, in a single-wide trailer that was one part wood for every three parts aluminum.

Every winter, the roof of its lean-to shack would crack and pop under the weight from the twenty-two inches of a Nicholas County snowfall. The old wood stove was never properly fitted at the top, causing flames to shoot out and streak overhead every time a log was thrown on. And orange-and-blue blazes danced perilously close to the Pink Panther fluffs of insulation that hung from the sagging ceiling above. When spring came, it rained just as hard inside as out, and the smell of mildew hung thick in the air long past the end of summer, clinging to your clothes and your very dignity. And I can tell you that long after the storm was over, those dark waters kept pouring down.

The floors were made of soggy pieces of particle board still soaked from the storms that ran ragged through a tin-metal roof the month before—boards that were now more or less being held together by the threadbare patches of a brown shag carpet hop-scotching its way across the living room floor, mere remnants of the days when the trailer was new. Now it was caked solid with a mix of old animal droppings and new chunks of mud every night from Dad's logging boots, until you couldn't tell where the brown carpet ended and the dirt began.

And . . . it was home.

When I tell people this thing about me, this preamble to who I am, you can see the uncomfortable sit upon their shoulders and start to get heavy. Like a weight they never asked to bear. They'll shift and unsettle and say things like, "Well, thank goodness you got out. Thank goodness that's not you anymore."

And that's where they would be wrong.

To be sure, I *hated* that trailer growing up. Hated everything about it. I would spend hours sitting outside with a pencil and a blue spiral-bound notebook, drawing sketches of it. Dreaming up ways to build walls around it. Put a roof over it. To somehow transform it, and therefore me and my future, overnight. I dreamed every day of what it would look like for our trailer to become a *real* house. As if that alone might give me a real chance at life.

"We could put beams all the way around the trailer, like spider's legs, right into the ground," I'd tell Mom when I showed her my sketches. "You could dig holes and pour concrete around them like you did for the swing set, and that would be enough to support a real roof."

I just knew that if I could come up with the right set of plans, a blueprint of sorts for the life I wanted to build, then Mom and Dad would catch the vision and I could bring them along with me. Could save them—from the world and from themselves, from the series of unfortunate decisions. And then we could build that good life together, side by side by side.

Or, if they couldn't or wouldn't be convinced, then I would just go out and build it myself.

So, yes, I have known since I was little that one way or another, whatever else I had to do to make it happen, I would get out of that trailer and make a different life for myself. But to say that's not me anymore—well, that's where you'd be wrong. Everything I am begins and returns to that trailer. And everywhere I go, whoever else it is that I've become along the way, I carry that trailer with me.

For me, this life—dug out and rebuilt from the ground up—has turned out to be much less a story about any kind of success than it is a song of redemption, a reconciliation with the roots that grew me, a melody born out of the muddiest parts of my life.

Because as for me and my story . . . it *always* started with dirt.

YEAR ROUND, I dumped scraps of brown beans and cornbread for the latest stray that had wandered into the yard. They were all kept in line by one feral gray tabby cat, who adopted me as its own when I was just four years old and found it abandoned at the old elementary schoolyard in New Hope. It came up to me purring, with its green eyes and the distinctive shape of an M in the fur on its forehead, which I took as a sign that we belonged together. So I wrapped that kitten in my favorite blanket and snuck it home, where I tentatively named it Thomas . . . until a year later when she had kittens and was henceforth and forevermore known as *Thomasina*.

We had a steady revolving door of stray dogs and cats turned temporary pets growing up, and none of them met a very happy ending. They would run away or disappear overnight, get hit by a truck that was going by a little too fast, get dropped off on the side of the road up some holler when we couldn't keep them, or get sick with what would have been a pretty curable fix if we ever actually took our animals to the vet. Instead they would die right where they lay, or once Mom called our neighbor next door—the one with the shotgun—and that was that.

"I hate to see an animal suffer," was all she said.

Those were the welcome kind of pets I knew growing up. But this trailer of ours had plenty of unwelcome ones as well. It was thick with mice in the winter and small roaches skittering all over everything in the summer. And often I'd even find the wiggling, churning, blanched-white bodies of maggots writhing in the kitchen sink and making a meal out of last week's dinner. I was nine years old the first time I figured out that if you poured a gallon of bleach directly on their little white bodies, they would curl up in a ball and die right where they lay. The magic of Clorox, indeed.

And, yes, being right in the thick of the wilds of West Virginia, there were plenty of wood snakes and brown snakes, and also the occasional rattlesnake. Once, when Dad and I were on the couch watching some show together, a big, fat, hissing snake came right over the top of the television at us, interrupting our programming indefinitely that night. I'm guessing it just wanted to watch a different channel, but I was pretty shook up nonetheless.

I can tell you right now, I was never sad when any of *them* met an unhappy ending. But the dogs and cats were a different story.

I think the hardest one ever was our black lab mix who had just had puppies. One of our neighbors put out a bowl of antifreeze for her—punishment for wandering into his yard once too often—and before we caught it she had passed it on to her nursing pups. In the space of one day, we lost them all. They curled up in a ball and died right where they lay. One by one, we laid them all out in the grass, silent and unmoving, until no hope was left. That was the first time I ever saw Dad cry. As he rocked that dog back and forth in his arms and buried his face in her sleek, black, bristly fur, the foam at her mouth mixing with the tears on his cheeks, I could hear him whispering, "*Don't go, don't go, don't go.*"

I knew right then this world sets out to hurt you.

And that was just the hand dealt from the decidedly indifferent God I thought I knew back then. A God who allowed suffering and would go along and let this house be fine and that house be fine, and then strike down the next one without any warning. He was the God who would stand by and let innocence be washed away in sheets . . . like the rain from a hot summer storm.

And I just knew, He was coming for me next.

GOD NEVER STARTED OUT for me as someone I feared.

In fact, the earliest memory I have of God is lying in bed at night, talking to Him through the windows in my room as He sat among the stars.

My bedroom was on one end of the trailer, where the farthest wall was made up of three threadbare aluminum windows that looked out toward Goldie's little red house. I say threadbare, because at the time not a one of those windows had a curtain or a blind on it. I guess back then I was still at an age where things didn't need to be kept hidden.

God could look right in on my life and see everything.

When darkness fell, and it was brighter outside than inside, it was as if the whole sky lit up like a silvery screen of stars. The windows were propped half open, and the warm summer air crawled in and curled up beside me. It brushed up against my bare legs, soft like fur, sighed, and settled in. I guess I was still at an age where things didn't need to be kept out either.

When the summer air couldn't sleep, it danced pirouettes on the blankets and twirled all around the room, floating freely and without fear on a current of innocence and security. I turned my face to the sky and talked to God just like He was a friend. And He, in turn, seemed to come down and hover just outside my window. His breath close enough to leave fog marks on the glass.

Goldie's little red house always still had a few lights on inside. And some nights I could see her walking around in there, her soft face glowing in the darkness. All the neighboring houses on our mountain were already dark—we were but a firefly in a vast distant sky—so on those nights it seemed as if there was no one else in the world but me and God. And sometimes Goldie.

This was not a God I ever remember anyone telling me about. This was not the wrathful God I would later meet in church, someone to be afraid of. And it was not the exclusive God I would later see some people make Him out to be, someone who told other people they didn't belong with Him. This was the God I seemed to have always known as a best friend, the one who came and visited me at my window. Face-to-face and free of fear. He was the God who drew close enough to leave marks across my life.

Long before anyone told me what He *should* be.

Shortly after that, God started meeting me outside in the yard during the daylight hours. When He wasn't in the stars, He was everywhere. He was in the green of the grass, down to the very pigment. He was in the birds stepping into flight, wings spread wide in defiance of gravity, far from the tether of their branches. He was in the sun shining down on my face, the kind of gold from the fire that you know is still there even when you close your eyes. He was in the way that thin layers of mud, once dug out from the cold, hard ground, would dry on your hands and stay with you the rest of the day. As if once it left its mark on you, you couldn't forget how it felt.

He was color and freedom and fire and dirt.

And His was the voice that told me someday all of this was going to make so much sense. He was going to use it all. The messy, the hard, the broken, the beautiful. One day He was going to put words to it. And then I'd see.

My story wouldn't be wasted.

2

you have to dig down to get to the good part

We shared a yard with Goldie.

Or rather, our trailer had been hauled in on an eighteen-wheeler flatbed truck and dropped on the back half of her property as a temporary solution that somehow turned permanent. So when you drove up Airport Road and made the first right down a dirt path driveway, it was Goldie's little two-bedroom, redwood-stained house that you saw up front facing the road, and our single-wide trailer—propped up on a precarious-looking pedestal of cinder blocks—the ever-unpleasant surprise waiting behind it. Eventually, Mom and Dad built on a porch and put up wood skirting all around the bottom to give it a more finished look. But it was still one of those "proximity problems with your in-laws" situations that seemed to make all parties involved equally unhappy.

The yard between our two houses was dotted with *stuff*. A pickup truck up on blocks, a pickup truck that actually worked, a 1970s Firebird Trans Am—gold with a giant eagle on the hood that seemed to actually fly when Aerosmith came on the radio. There was a camper, a loader, the occasional dozer that came caked to the blade four inches deep with mud. And for a few years before the bank came and took it away from us, a boat that had belonged to my Grandpa Bill before he went and died. There was a random pile of scrap metal, a bonfire pit—which was really just a burnt spot on the grass that never seemed to stop smoking—and old rubber tires that Mom had painted white and used to plant wildflowers in random places all around the yard. There was a toolshed, a wood-shed, an old cinder block garage, and on the weekends, our Mack and Kenworth big rigs parked right there in the grass.

To keep the Mack and Kenworth from rolling too far into the yard, Dad brought home a bunch of dirt left over from digging out the latest log road and shaped it into a wedge of sorts—a three-foot-tall blunt barrier on one end that sloped off to a gentle decline on the other. When the trucks were parked there, they rested right up against that three-foot edge. But in the spring, when the grass grew in and the trucks were out hauling logs and the rain created little puddles up and down the ramp, us kids in the neighborhood would ride our bikes up the incline as fast as we could and go flying off the edge like the superheroes we always knew we were, shouting "By the power of Grayskull!" as our bikes flew through the air. You have to be *committed* to the ramp. I dubbed that mound of mud "Mountain Spring" in honor of all the puddles, and named myself its heir apparent.

Queen Mary, ruler of the dirt.

Even when the bank came and took both the Kenworth and the Mack and left us with no big rigs in need of stopping, Mountain Spring still lived on in their absence. Until a few years later when Dad finally broke over and bulldozed it down to make room for a new pile of gravel.

And then I became Queen Mary, ruler of the rocks.

You have to be willing to *adapt* as your story changes.

EVERY APRIL, when the thick carpet of rotten leaves in the woods around our house gave way to a flash of green, Goldie would send me packing with a spade and an empty bucket and tell me not to come back until it was full.

"Don't just cut the leaves, Mary Ellen. You got to dig down to get to the good part."

I had the route memorized by heart. From the top of our mountain we had woods in every direction, so for shorthand we called it the woods in front of our trailer and the woods behind. This path led me to the woods in front. Quick over the hill and down three levels of logging roads, veer a hard left at the first waterfall (the one with the fallen tree), skitter down where the ground is nothing but rocks (it's easier if you crawl), and then, just as the hill drops off in a steep, sheer cliff, you should be able to see it: a secret patch of ramps that was just mine and Goldie's.

A ramp is a kind of wild onion that grows thick, deep in the woods where I come from. In fact, the town of Richwood at the bottom of Fenwick Mountain is so well-known for them that it's called the ramp capital of the world, and every year they host a festival called the Feast of the Ramson. But as for us, our feast always took place at home.

When I got back, Goldie was already hard at work making brown beans and cornbread and frying up bacon in the pan. She'd take that bucket of greens from me, rinse the dirt off more or less, and then fry them up right there in that pan with the bacon grease.

Here's something you need to know if you're going to eat ramps: you'll smell like them for three solid days after. Not just on your breath, not just up close—it will ooze right out of your pores. The only way to deal with it is for everyone in the house to eat them so you don't have to smell each other. You have to be *committed* to the ramp.

Years later, when I was in law school in New Haven, I went to a fancy restaurant with white linen tablecloths and real cloth napkins. And wouldn't you know it, they had wild ramps right there on the menu—called it French and gourmet. I ordered them, of course, but I can tell you right now: that fancy French place had nothing on West Virginia Goldie and her dirty bacon grease.

We had all sorts of interesting meals like that growing up. Like the deer meat the men who worked for Dad would give us every hunting season. Dad was never a hunter himself—I think he lacked the killer instinct—but he sure wouldn't let that meat go to waste. So Goldie would fry it up in the pan and boil some green beans with yet more bacon, and it tasted just like tough, gamey hamburger that had been cooked a little too long. But it was food on the table, so we didn't complain.

Sometimes the hunting season was squirrel, so we'd go ahead and eat that too. Goldie turned it into a thick gravy with large chunks of squirrel meat—greasy like dark chicken—and poured it over white bread. I always hated that meal the most. I think it's because at one time or another, we had a pet squirrel.

Dad found it hurt in a tree he had cut down, so he brought that squirrel home to heal and we named it Hector. He would sit on my shoulder and hide under my hair, and we'd feed him cracked walnuts and stale popcorn. When he got better and started running crazy all over the house, Dad took him back to the woods and released him into the wild.

And just in time, too, because not long after that he found a nest of baby flying squirrels whose mama must have been hurt or killed, or maybe just abandoned them outright as sometimes happens. So he brought them on home, and we fed them with eyedroppers until they were strong enough to be set free too.

It was confusing to say the least.

We loved them as our pets. But come squirrel season, you can bet we still had that gravy.

You have to be willing to adapt as your *situation* changes too.

THE NAMES we give things have power.

Goldie Philistine King was born smack-dab in the middle of a total of thirteen children her parents brought into the world.

Besides her, there were Lee and Gerald, Bernell and Harold, Lena and Edith and Ann. The twins—Dora Lee and Ora Lee—one who died at birth, the other who spent most of her adult life confined to a wheelchair in a nursing home from an illness that could readily be treated today. There was Hilbert, who had one arm, and another sibling I'm not sure I ever knew the name of. And then there was her sister Tressie, who ran off to California when she was old enough and never looked back.

If you want to know how Goldie's father felt about her, you need look no further than her own middle name. If you were to look up *philistine* in the dictionary right now, you'd see it means uncultured, unknowledgeable. I've always wondered what kind of parent would label their child uneducated before she even had a chance to learn. One who saw very little value in girl-children, I'm assuming. And Goldie hinted on more than one occasion that when her dad spent time with the bottle, she was one of those he took it out on the most.

But one thing she was never subtle about was just how much she *hated* that middle name.

As for me, I just always knew her as Grandma Goldie.

One part firecracker, one part sassafras.

On Sundays at church, she wore a pink suit, high-collar lace shirt, and White Shoulders lady perfume. But back home in jeans and a T-shirt, she could slam a door like nobody's business.

Her favorite sayings were "I'll do it myself!" and "When in Rome, do as the Romans do . . . and in case you missed it, *I'm the dang Roman!*"

At five foot, two inches tall, she was a towering force in our family tree. A tough woman born of tough Scotch-Irish stock who had lived a brutal life. She was not afraid to get her hands dirty. She was forever out working in the yard, elbow deep in the dirt, planting her beloved butterfly bushes, as if always trying to summon some sort of transformation.

Instead of waiting on any man in our family to fix something, she got out there and fixed it herself. At least once a week, you'd see

her marching down over the hill, shovel in hand and swearing under her breath, to dig out our sewer, which was really just a pipe that emptied directly into the woods and had a tendency of backing up.

Goldie had short, curly, soft, brown-turned-gray hair that she used to get permed once a month into tiny ringlets at the beauty parlor. But now it had turned into a dandelion puff of untamed mane, no matter how many times a day she combed it. She wore large round glasses—the kind that turn dark in the sun—on top of her even rounder face. But if you looked close enough, you could see her gray-blue eyes laughing behind them. And when she smiled, she had these big apple cheeks sitting high on her cheekbones.

Big apple cheeks that she shared with me.

She wore full dentures and would take them out every night and put them in a cup of water on the coffee table in the living room, where they stood guard for her until morning. Eventually, she ended up with a touch of skin cancer on the end of her nose, so the doctor cut it off—the tip of her nose to save her face—and every time she turned to the side you could see that it ended in an abrupt hard edge where round used to be.

When she got it in her mind to do something, there was no slowing her down. Like that summer when I was nine and she decided the old garage that stood between her house and our trailer needed to come down. She said she'd take it down herself cinder block by cinder block if she had to. So she hooked a rusty log chain to the second-floor window and tied the other end to her old silver Chevy pickup truck, intending to pull out just the frame. But as soon as she hit that gas, just a little too hard I guess, the entire building came down in one big, scrapping heap with a great boom that rattled the windows and shook the entire mountain.

When she crawled out of that truck to see what she had done, she stared at me in shock, her eyebrows raised so high they looked like two bees stuck in her dandelion hair.

And then she said, "Well, Mary Ellen, *that's one way to get the job done!*"

She spent the rest of the summer hauling that building off to the dump cinder block by cinder block. But come fall, you can bet the job was finished. She was the first one to show me that if you want something in this world, you don't wait on anyone else to hand it to you.

You do it yourself.

Yes, Goldie Bess was a force to be reckoned with.

And she was also my best friend.

THERE'S THIS SCENE in the movie *Steel Magnolias*.

Sally Field is there in the cemetery after she's just lost Shelby, and she's talking to the other women about how beautiful it is to witness an entire life, start to finish. To be there when someone drifts into your life and to still be holding on to their hand when they drift back out. I know that's meant to be about death and loss, but I think it also tells us something pretty powerful about how to look at our own life too.

In any life, there are going to be some scenes we want to delete. Some that we want to fast-forward through or rewind to get right. There are scenes we're afraid will be too hard for other people to look at. Scenes that we're afraid will end up hurting someone else if we include them in the final edit at all.

But we forget just how beautiful it is to witness an entire life, start to finish.

Here's what I know: Those parts of us that we want to hide. Those parts of us that we wish we could bury below the surface far away from the light, praying for transformation. Those things we think will make people turn their faces away from us in some sort of sympathy shame on our behalf.

For better or worse, those things help make us who we are.

We need to roll up our sleeves and get busy about the work of digging into that. We need to get our hands into it. Feel the hard ground break up and shake loose at our unflinching willingness to hold on. To look closer. To see what we didn't see before.

Goldie was right.

Sometimes you do have to dig down to get to the good part.

When I look back on my life, I have a decision to make. Will I see only mud on the surface, or will I also see the miracle underneath?

Will I believe that all along I was alone in it, that it really was always up to me to *do* for myself? Or will I believe that Someone else was always there holding my hand?

A face that drew close to mine and never once turned away.

No matter how far I drifted.

a tiny shift in words
that changes everything

WHEN I THINK OF MY MOTHER, I think of her dirty, bare feet.

In the first few years of my life, Dad went to work and Mom stayed home with me. She'd make me frozen fish sticks and serve pink lemonade in a canning jar. She'd sit me down in front of the TV, where I would watch *Winnie the Pooh* and stay in my nightgown until warm afternoon light poured in through the windows. Then she would turn the radio up, and I'd watch her dance a hip-swaying slow dance to a country song as she held on to a broom and glided across our kitchen floor, making mismatched piles of chevron-shaped mud, her bare feet standing in the leftover tracks from Dad's boots the night before.

The whole room started to glow golden, as if lit from beneath and bathed in brilliant light. The dust stirred up from the broom became glittered, gilded flecks floating on an ethereal, ebbing, invisible current that never seemed to land. For a moment, it felt as though all three of us—Mom, me, and Thomasina the cat—were buoyed up there, floating on a cloud of glittering dirt. Our bare feet not touching the ground at all. And Mom still hip-swaying to the music all around us.

Those were the golden days of my childhood. Everything was warm. Everything was slow. Everything was light. And I was *safe, safe, safe.*

When Dad came home from work, he liked to tousle my hair on the top of my head and call me The Kid.

"How's The Kid doing today?"

"What did The Kid get up to today?"

"Hey Kidster, come here and talk to your ol' dad for a minute."

The Kid, Kid, Kidster.

The entire time I was growing up, I don't remember a single time—unless he was talking to a teacher or some other adult—that my father ever called me by my given name. To him, I was The Kid.

The Kid was me.

Which was extra confusing, considering he was also the one who named me.

DAD HAD NEVER REALLY WANTED KIDS, at least as far as his twenty-three years of life had taken him. Mom liked to remind me of this often. That she was the one who wanted me, the one who fought to start a family.

"You know, if it had been left up to your dad," she said, "you wouldn't be here now."

Dad didn't understand kids. Didn't much like them. They cried, they needed things, they weren't really all that interesting. He had already become a young husband, and now here he was being rushed into becoming a father. And he wanted no part of it. For the first nine months, in fact, every time Mom asked him to feel her belly or show any kind of interest at all, he had none to offer.

In the hospital, while everything was still all pink balloons and pink blankets, Dad ran out to buy some celebratory cigars. Not because he smoked at all, and not because he was feeling especially celebratory, but because that was what you did when a new baby came into the world in the 1980s: smoke cigars with all the men in the hospital waiting room.

While he was gone, Mom decided that she was going to name me Renata Ann. She told the nurse and made it official. But when JR Bess returned, cigars in hand, he decided Renata Ann sounded way too much like Ramada Inn. And by God, no kid of his was going to be named after a hotel chain.

So right there on the spot, he changed my name.

He chose Mary, after his favorite aunt, and for the middle name he chose one after his own grandmother. And that was that: *Mary Ellen*. He named me after two solid, good, honest women who weren't afraid of hard work. Because he knew that the life he had in mind for me was going to require a lot of it.

Goldie always loved to tell me this next part.

She took him by the arm and they slow-walked down the hallway to where all the new babies are put on display in their tiny plastic beds, lined up one after another. Before they had even rounded the corner, Dad could hear all the babies crying.

He rolled his eyes in a huff. "Listen at that racket. I bet *that kid* of mine is the one in there crying the loudest, just leading the bunch of 'em."

"Now, Junior, you don't know that."

And sure enough, when they rounded that corner—at least as far as the truth according to Grandma Goldie is concerned—I was the only baby in the entire room who wasn't making a sound. I was just looking around, wide-eyed, wondering what all the fuss was about.

And just like that, the cold, hard ground beneath my Dad's heart warmed and shifted. And I went from being "that kid" to "The Kid" from then on after.

A tiny shift in words that meant everything had changed in his heart.

By the time I was four, Goldie started taking me with her to church every week for Sunday school.

Six days out of the week I would be out in a T-shirt and shorts, scrambling up some crabapple tree with skinned, bloody knees or hanging upside down from the top bar of the yellow-and-brown swing set in our yard. Not the regular hanging bar that came with it, mind you, but the very tippy-top crossbar that held the whole thing together. I would stand on the plastic horse swing—when I wasn't using it to play *She-Ra, Princess of Power*—and pull myself up on the trapeze bar on the far left side. From there, I could use my momentum to flip my legs way up in the air so they would catch on the highest part of the swing set, and I could let my arms dangle down toward the ground. I hung upside down like that for what felt like hours, the blood gloriously rushing to my increasingly purple face. My T-shirt flipped up way over my head. Laughing deliriously for no apparent reason, other than doing what they said couldn't be done.

"Kid, get down from there!" Dad always *hated* it when I did this. "You're going to break your fool neck."

But then he'd go back inside and leave me to it.

Six days out of the week I was a wild thing, a blur of climbed trees and skinned knees and doing what I wasn't supposed to. *Untamed.*

But on the *seventh* day, Goldie would make sure I was in the frilliest pink dress she could find. She'd make me put on a white Easter hat and gloves, even though it was just a regular ol' Sunday. And we went to church like the proper, prim ladies we were.

At least *one* day out of the week.

"God's drawing down His eyes at you right now, Mary Ellen."

Goldie would always tell me this anytime I put up a protest about going to church. Or tried to put up a protest about doing anything, really. Apparently, hers was a version of God that seemed quick to be displeased.

My attendance was required, a nonnegotiable. But Dad never had to go with us to church on Sunday. He would either go to work or park himself on the couch to watch TV and not move a muscle all day. On those days, he took the *sabbath* part of Sunday very seriously. But though he never went, that didn't stop him from wanting me to be the best I could be in school, even if it was just Sunday school.

Like that Christmas, when the whole mountain packed into the Macedonia Methodist Church for one evening to watch the annual children's Christmas program. I was not yet five years old and wouldn't be starting kindergarten for another nine months, but Dad got it into his head that I should stand up in front of the whole sanctuary and recite—*rote from memory*—the entire length of "'Twas the Night Before Christmas."

On stage. By myself. In front of a packed church.

When Dad got something into his head that he thought I should do, there was no point fighting him. I just went ahead and did it.

So for weeks we practiced that poem. Him sitting at the kitchen table with me, his giant hands clasped over the book, the mud still caked into the creases and folds of his flannel shirt leaving marks all across the pages. Just listening to those words over and over again. And any time I so much as stumbled over a syllable, I had to start over all the way back from the beginning.

"Do it again," he'd say.

To him, it wasn't enough that I memorized it, wasn't enough that I recited it alone—it needed to be *perfect*.

On the night of the Christmas program, Mom put me in a little red velvet dress with lace around the collar that she probably found at a yard sale the summer before. The scabs on my skinned knees were showing through the white tights that went with it, and my black buckled shoes didn't even reach the ground as I sat swinging my feet, scared to death from my place in the front pew. The church was dark except for one bright pin spotlight from the back. But even in the darkness, I could see there wasn't an empty seat in the entire house, and there were rows of people standing all along the back.

The older kids played out scenes of Mary and Joseph, a manger, some angels, then they sang Christmas carols. I always wanted to be an angel because they got to wear the silver tinsel halos and white choir robes and looked so very grown up. But instead I was stuck in red velvet, a little kid just waiting for my turn.

When they called me up to that stage, you couldn't hear a sound. There was just me, a spotlight, and a fifty-six-line divide between where I stood and making Dad proud of me. The light in my eyes made it so I couldn't see faces in the crowd, except one. His back was straight like an arrow, his giant hands folded in his lap. His eyes were fixed straight ahead with a look that said it all:

"Don't fidget, and don't mess it up."

And at four years old, without ever stumbling over a single word, I recited that poem start to finish from the front of the Macedonia Methodist Church.

If for no other reason than Dad *also* loved our family doing what others said couldn't be done.

IT WENT SO WELL that the following year Dad decided I should do it again, this time reciting "'Twas the Night Before Jesus Came." Which is a real thing. Only this time I didn't practice as hard. Didn't feel like sitting down to memorize it. And when I got up on stage, twice I had to be reminded by the lady in charge of the show what the next line was.

In other words, in my eyes, I had *failed*. Twice.

After the show, each of the kids opened one present that their parents brought from home to put under the tree that night. But not me. I sat alone on the edge of that stage, staring at my shiny, black buckled shoes that I had just about outgrown, my head hanging low. Afraid to look into my father's eyes.

"Well, Kid, aren't you going to open your present?" He towered over me in his only gray suit.

"That was for only if I didn't mess up. And I did. *Twice*."

He quietly handed me the last box under the tree. "Well, I'll tell you what. This gift wasn't for how you did. This gift is just because your ol' dad loves you."

Though I wouldn't realize it for years to come, that night at the Macedonia Methodist Church was the first time I ever got a glimpse of the God I would one day come to know: not the one drawing down His eyes at me, quick to be displeased. Not a God withholding love, just waiting to see how I perform. But a good Father.

We never have to be afraid to look up into His face, no matter how short we feel like we've fallen again and again. Because the gifts He has for us are never dependent on how well or how much we do, but always simply because He loves us.

And no amount of messing up can ever change that.

Like I said, it would take me *years* to fully understand that.

And in the meantime, that wasn't going to stop JR Bess from making sure I always did the best I could in school.

Because in his drawn and weary eyes, it was my only way out.

As KINDERGARTEN loomed on the horizon, Dad was first and foremost determined that I wouldn't be the *dimmest* one in class.

It was a feeling he had known all too well when he first started grade school at New Hope Elementary—the same schoolyard where we found Thomasina the cat, and the very same school I would be attending that fall. It was a small, five-room schoolhouse, just big enough that every two grades had to be combined in order to make it work. Kindergarten and first grade were together in one room, third and fourth in another, and fifth and sixth took up the room opposite the lunchroom turned gymnasium. Second grade inexplicably got a room all to themselves.

And there it stood waiting for me, unchanged, just as it had been for him.

This legacy of *limited* education.

It sat up on a hill right next door to the Macedonia Methodist Church. The same little steepled church where Goldie had taken Dad to Sunday school every week when he was a boy. The same Sunday school she insisted on taking me to now.

Not a lot of things had changed on our mountain in a generation.

But Dad was determined one thing would.

When he was in school there, he had been constantly laughed at and picked on in class for how unprepared and falling behind he was. And that forever branded him. It burned in his brain as the proof that he was never cut out to be anything more in this life than—in his words—a "dumb ol' logger."

But by God, his daughter would be more.

So he started bringing home workbooks, the kind they sold on racks near the cash register at the grocery store. I remember staring at them every time I went in with Mom—right there next to the Bubble Yum—because they had a picture of a kid on the front cover that was made entirely out of dots and symbols and letters in a very dot-matrix-printing, child-of-the-eighties sort of way. They were ranked by grade in school, and you could get them for either math or reading. The obvious presumption was that you would get your child the workbook for whatever grade they were going into.

But Dad was never big on presumptions.

He started me in the kindergarten workbooks for sure, but he didn't stop there. Every night when he came home, I had to sit at the kitchen table after dinner and work through math and reading problems for hours on end, while the sounds of Jack and Chrissy and Janet on *Three's Company* floated in from the other room. When I finished a workbook, he would just bump me up another grade. So that by the time I actually entered Mrs. Oliver's kindergarten class that fall, Dad felt like I was finally pretty close to being prepared.

I was at a fifth-grade math and sixth-grade reading level.

WHEN WE WEREN'T WORKING on workbooks together, Dad had me read the encyclopedia. It was one of those thirty-volume sets that were sold door to door, where when you couldn't afford the whole set all at once, you would pay by the book on the installment plan. I can still remember Mom getting a new one in the mail each month and adding it to the shelf beside its alphabetical seatmate. "Metamorphosis to New Jersey" slid in right next to "Livingstone to Metalwork."

Dad knew that's just how it goes: education was a luxury for poor people, doled out in begrudging scraps at a cost made much higher over time. But he also saw it as the key to getting out, a "Legacy to Logger" if you will, wrapped up in the pages of a gilded bound book.

We would stand on the porch together, stepping out from under the shadow of the old wooden overhang, and look up at a blanket of indigo sky embroidered with celestial bodies in constellations. From the top of our mountain, you can see every star.

For hours he had me memorize the names of stars and the moon's rotation around an earth that was in turn spinning wildly around the sun. When I got those two backwards, as I often did, my frustrated father would lose his temper with me. He'd huff and ask how hard it was to remember.

"Kid, exactly how many times do you have to be told before you'll learn?"

But I think for him the real frustration was that he was offering me—and I was taking for granted—something he was never afforded: an education. The space to study and learn and look only to the skies for my limits. The option to be more than just a dot on the map in the constellation of mountains where I come from.

Dad grew up in a time when an Ohio boy named John Glenn orbited the earth three times and President Kennedy challenged every American to put a man on the moon. And then he watched in awe as they did. He had been obsessed with the space program from that moment forward.

I think it was the first time he realized that we can be more than where we're from. That it's possible to go further than where we started. And it was the first time he realized there had been no one in his life to challenge him to do the same. He always wondered what would have happened—how life would have turned out differently for him—if there had been.

It was the one kind of challenge that he vowed would never be missing from my life.

So every night I worked in thick workbooks at our tiny, semi-attached, prefab kitchen table. And I was the heir to my father's education long before I ever started school. So that when I started kindergarten that fall at least five grades ahead of the curve, they used words like *smart . . . bright . . . well ahead of her class*. Even talked about having me skip a grade.

At one point a few years later, they sent my teacher, Mrs. Barrett, out to the house to talk about having me put in a special gifted program. But when she knocked on the door, Goldie got it backwards, misunderstanding what she was saying.

"Listen, Mary Ellen's no dummy," she said. "She oughtta at least be able to stay with her class. She'll learn to keep up."

There was just something about Goldie, and the Appalachia she was brought up in, where she always expected the worst to come knocking at the door.

But once Mrs. Barrett explained again, there was a week of interviews and IQ tests and puzzles with blocks they gave me to play with while a man with a clipboard observed. And after that, one day a week, I and six other kids would leave our regular class to be given the gift of an advanced education.

And those labels became a lifeline.

A lens through which I started to see my life for everything that it could be and not just what it was. It started to *change* everything. Words have the power to speak life or death. When they call you smart, you act smart. You play up or down to what is expected of you.

And when it came to Dad, there was never any question: *much* was expected of me.

But if there's anything those early days studying the encyclopedia taught me, it's this:

Long before *metamorphosis* comes *logger* and *legacy*.

And those nights spent getting the education Dad always wanted would speak *volumes* of transformation in my life for years to come.

marked for hard things

JR BESS CAME BURSTING into the world, down at the Sacred Heart Hospital in the middle of town, mid-December in the mid-1950s, sometime around midnight.

In such a hurry was he to make his way into the world, that a nurse had to lie across Goldie's legs to keep her from delivering long enough so the doctor could be woken up in time to get there. Goldie told me that story—the nurse, the legs, the absentee doctor—so many times I could tell it myself. And each time she did, all I could think was, how on earth was this larger-than-life giant of a man I knew as my father ever contained in such a tiny woman's body?

I guess he couldn't be, and that was the point.

Dad had the typical first few years of childhood for a boy born in the 1950s. Almost as if there was some sort of kit being handed out by hospitals back then, along with little blue blankets and a note that read, "Here, you'll be needing this over the next five or six years." And so as I flip through the pages of time and one maroon leather photo album, there are the predictable black-and-white photos staring back at me.

And I look into the face of a version of my father I have never known.

There are tiny squares filled frame to frame with images of a freckle-faced boy with ears too big for his head, which in turn is too big for his little body. There's a gap between his two front teeth—the same gap I would one day inherit—just big enough for the trouble to get in. And he smiles without a flash of the worry or weary I have since grown to know clouding his gray-green-turned-monochrome eyes. Here he's wearing a plaid button-down short sleeve shirt and a cowboy hat with a string tied under his little chin. Here he is at Gatlinburg. Here he's out in front of a Cherokee reservation.

Once my father was someone who saw big things in this world.

As I turn the page, the pictures tell a story. Around age twelve he starts to disappear from the frames, with only his annual school photo—the same crew cut, the same gray-green background—to mark the passing of time.

Dad was just twelve years old when he went to work in the woods.

I guess the mountain I come from was never easy on *anyone*.

The twenty-five miners in the Saxsewell No. 8 mine can't see a way out.

It's the early morning hours of a May that feels more like March, and despite the sun now falling brightly on the glinting rocks outside, deep in the belly and bowels of the mountain, where the light can no longer find you, it's *always* the dead of night. Only a slurry of slow-motion seconds before, the continuous miner machine—a mechanized locust with grit for teeth—chewed its way into a flooded and abandoned auxiliary line. And now a rush of black water has been unleashed in a torrent through the main artery of the mine, a muddy mixture of coal dust, sweat, and broken promises.* In an instant, it fills up their only way out . . . and their burning,

---

*Information gathered in part from "May 6, 1968: Incident at Hominy Falls Traps 25 Miners for Days," West Virginia Public Broadcasting, May 6, 2019, https://www .wvpublic.org/post/may-6-1968-incident-hominy-falls-traps-25-miners-days #stream/0.

on-fire lungs are left gasping for air and begging for a final reprieve. Four of the men are killed instantly. Twenty-one others sit in the silent, freezing, coal-black darkness, waiting for a lifeline that may never come.

IN THE SPRING OF 1968, when Dad was eleven going on twelve, both my grandpa Bill and his brother, Dad's uncle Cleon, were working full shifts in the West Virginia coal mines. For Grandpa Bill, that was in addition to working in the woods. He got up and was off to work by five o'clock every morning, put in ten or twelve good hours cutting logs, came home to grab a quick dinner and a change of shirt, and went back out again to work the evening shift in the mines, all before bedtime. And then he'd wake up and do it all over again the next day. Grandpa Bill put in two hard days of work in the time it took most men in this world to think about doing one.

Work ethic is the one inheritance in our family we've never had to worry about whether we could lay claim to.

Way back in Hominy Falls on the southern side of Nicholas County, where the road switchbacks so hard up and down the mountain that you can swing around and kiss your taillights with every twisting turn, if you'll follow that road long enough, eventually the steep hillside gives way to open quarry. There, in the ghostly white limestone graveyard—a scooped-out, hollow underbelly of dirt disemboweled from earth, where only the shells remain of the men they once were—was where you'd find a company of miners known as the Gauley Coal and Coke Saxsewell No. 8 mine.

There they were guarded by a legion of antiquated iron dinosaurs—part relic, part machine called a "tipple"—with belts running up and down their spines where spikes and scales should have been. Around the clock, those conveyor belts churned out a steady stream of coal—*bituminous black gold*—climbing higher and higher out of the guts of the mountain until it dropped some twenty feet into the waiting coal trucks below.

In another five or ten years, the next phase of the machinery revolution would send some 70 percent of the state's miner workforce home to their wild-eyed wives and hungry kids, eventually kicking off one of the biggest downward spirals into widespread poverty that a region had ever seen. Their only severance: a handshake, a thank-you, and a likely case of black lung from all the dust that still hadn't settled over those machines. But until then, coal was an underground kingdom rich for the taking, and the coal miner its loyal subject.

Grandpa Bill worked at a different mine in a different part of the county in those days. He wasn't among the colony of men with hard hats and head lamps heading off to the tunnels that morning of May 6, looking more like marching ants ready to till the soil than grown men just trying to feed their families.

So he wasn't there when all hell broke loose.

IT WAS COLD the morning of the accident—the kind of cold where you could see your breath in pure white puffs of vapor—as the day crew huddled over their metal lunch boxes and hot thermoses of coffee and prepared to get even colder upon descending into the mountain. That deep in the earth, it made no difference how warm it was outside. Where they were going there was only dark and damp and dust and cold waiting for them. It was a thankless job, the kind of doubled-over, doubled-down decision that takes eighteen-year-old boys and churns them into old men well before their time. If it doesn't kill them first. The Saxsewell No. 8 mine at Big Sewell Mountain never had a problem swallowing grown men whole. The only question was whether or not it would see fit to spit them back out again come the end of the day.

The shift before, Cleon was the one operating the continuous miner as it chewed and ground its way perilously close to that flooded auxiliary shaft. But then the whistle blew and the shifts changed, and that Monday morning it was another man operating the machine, while Cleon was assigned to a different part of the mine entirely, one much closer to the surface. And so it was that the random lottery of time cards and work assignments meant it was another man, and not Cleon, who was a mile deep into the mountain when the floodgates opened. That man was one of the four killed instantly. And Cleon was one of the twenty-one who had no other choice but to sit, to wait . . . and to pray.

FOR TEN DAYS, rescuers—including Grandpa Bill, who told his own mine foreman not to count on him coming back until his brother was safe and back home—continued pumping out water and inching their way further and further down into the mine.

The twenty-one trapped and praying men had been separated by the flood into two distinct groups. Fifteen of them, including Cleon, huddled together in a pocket of air and hope much closer to the surface, where they could hear the sound of rescue efforts underway. The remaining six—who were by then presumed dead—were sacrificed to the deepest parts of the mine. For *ten days* those men suffered with very little food and dirty water, sitting in the dark and the cold alongside the even colder bodies of the four men who weren't so lucky. They huddled together for warmth, made blankets out of their work coats, and spoke in hushed tones about the families they might never see again.

For ten days, an eleven-going-on-twelve version of my dad stood watch over the rescue efforts. He waited. He hoped. And he did what he could to help. The Red Cross was on the scene, churning out a steady stream of sandwiches, which they put on the belts of those iron dinosaurs, now moving in reverse, sending precious fuel back *into* the mine. Dad was given the task of fashioning metal tubes out of aluminum piping to carry the sandwiches and make them heavy enough so they wouldn't fall off the belt.

Why is it that sometimes the things we need most can only get to us in the form of carrying heavy things?

He would help move the hoses and run and get things when the rescuers needed them. But mostly he stood. He watched. He waited. And he kept hope alive. For days, he watched other men crawl out of that hole, black dust covering every inch of them, blinking as they made their way into the blinding light to stand in a ghostly white graveyard.

On day six, rescuers broke through to the first fifteen. When Cleon finally emerged to the surface, almost unrecognizable from the coating of coal dust all over him, Dad was the first one there waiting and went running up to hug him. And when Cleon hugged him back, fighting hard to hold back tears from the family he thought he'd never see again, it left one carbon copy coal handprint on the back of a little boy's coat.

On day ten, when they had all but given up hope, one of the rescuers happened to see a fresh footprint—proof of life—and the efforts were ramped up once more. When they finally broke through and found those six men huddled together and holding on for dear life, it was dubbed the Miracle at Hominy Falls.

Goldie loved to tell me that story. Her gray-blue eyes would light up when she stretched out that word "*mir-a-cle*" a second longer than she had to. She even claimed to still have that coat with the perfectly preserved handprint tucked away in a closet somewhere. I think for her it was like having a real artifact from heaven: *a shroud marked by a man who was once entombed.*

For her, it was proof positive that there is a God and He is *good* and He cares deeply about whether or not we are making our way home and the heavy, *heavy* things we carry.

But for me, I always secretly wondered if that wasn't the day Dad was marked—like some sort of working-man's-hands osmosis through a little boy's tan Carhartt coat—for a lifetime of hard work and hard luck and hard things.

And if that was how that worked, I just knew: I didn't want those hands on me.

WHENEVER DAD TOLD THIS STORY, his eyes always softened, retreated into their sockets, and went distant, like he wasn't so much looking at me anymore but *before* me to a scene replaying itself in broken monochrome sepia somewhere in the space that existed between where he had been and where I was going.

"All's I remember is that it was *so* cold and I was *so* hungry."

I would press him on the details. How long the rescue took. What kind of jobs they gave him to help out with. But no matter where the conversation went, it always returned to this.

SoHungrySoColdSoHungrySoCold.

When he said it, you could actually feel him shiver at the words. Like it wasn't so much something he was remembering as something he was reliving. I leaned in. What was it about the being cold, what was it about the being hungry? And why is that the part he remembered the most?

"Well, see, the Red Cross was up there handing out sandwiches to everybody. But me being just a boy, I didn't understand that they was *free* for everybody. And my dad always taught me, 'Boy, you don't take anything but what you can pay for.'"

"Right. Okay." I waited, letting him fill the silence.

"Yeah, well, so everybody's up there eating all around me, and I haven't had a bite to eat in fifteen hours or so. And it's cold, it's *so* cold. And Dad's somewhere down deep in the mine there, trying to dig out Cleon. So nobody knows I'm still up there, nobody knows I haven't eaten."

I nodded at this, even though he wasn't really looking at me.

"So I think to myself, I could just take one of those sandwiches.

Take just one. Could take it and pay 'em back later and they'd never know the difference. But *then* I think to myself, 'If I take even one of those sandwiches, though, it's just like I'm taking it right out of the hands of one of those trapped miners.'"

At this he always choked up and swallowed back the words like he had a mouthful of dirt and rocks.

"And I was *so cold and so hungry.* And all I could think was how much colder and how much hungrier all those men must be. Trapped down there like animals. Dad. And Cleon."

We stared at each other a long time at this, those words hanging in the space between us. Between where he had been and where I was going. Both fighting with everything we had to hold back a flood of tears.

"And I just knew. I didn't want to wind up down there, *trapped* in the mines like them."

it was always in our blood

For Dad, the events at Hominy Falls over those ten days were a turning point in his life.

Boys his age growing up in rural West Virginia at that time had mostly two choices for what they could do after high school: go to the mines or go to the woods. College wasn't even part of the conversation. And you need only take one look at the obituaries of those dead men who never got to be part of the miracle in Hominy that day to see how that played out.

"Mr. Dodd was 42 years of age and had 24 years mining experience . . ."

"Mr. McClung was 46 years of age and had 27 years mining experience . . ."

All of them survived by a widow and their two . . . three . . . five dependent children.

These young men—eighteen and nineteen when they first started crawling into the mines—had already worked a lifetime by the time they were in their forties. And as it turned out, that was all the lifetime they had to give.

Right around the time of the disaster in Hominy, Grandpa Bill had been offered the opportunity to lease a bunch of mining equipment and start his own independent operation. But after pulling his brother from the belly of Big Sewell Mountain, he turned down the offer and purchased a bulldozer instead. Named this new enterprise of his Bess Logging Company.

By that summer, and before he had quite turned twelve, Dad was out in the woods working with him.

Growing up, I had always assumed Dad never had any choice in the matter about going to work in the woods. That he had been forced into it at such a young age and told things like, "Now you go to work. Your place is in the woods. Forget about the future. Forget about college. Forget about anything else you had planned. This is your place now. Taking care of your family." That he was only twelve years old when his fate had been sealed for him.

But as it turned out, to him logging *did* feel like a choice. It felt like getting out.

When he was out there in the woods and could spend time with his dad, could play with what he thought of as oversized Tonka toys in the form of a bulldozer, could look up and see blue sky above him, could breathe fresh, clean air . . . that didn't feel like a life sentence to him. That didn't feel trapped.

That job felt like freedom.

And he was more than happy to go *outside* and work.

ONE OF DAD'S FIRST-EVER JOBS in the woods was to put the timber grabs—two giant hooks on a hinge like a pair of scissors—into the logs that had just been cut, so they could be pulled down to the landing by the horses.

Horses. Like it was still 1869.

Every time Dad tells me this part of the story, I make him slow down and repeat it just to be sure. Logging is one of those industries—a family tradition frozen in time—that hasn't changed much over the years. At least not the way Dad does it: *one man, one saw, for every one tree at a time.* He's a man who still believes that one of the greatest failings a logger can ever commit is having the gall to down one of these hundred-year-old giants only to bust it up into a million splinters when it hits the ground.

So he *whispers* to the trees when he's out there. Talks to them. Asks them what they need to "*Get on over!*" safely. And the trees talk back to him. He hears the whispers of his ancestors through their leaves when the wind blows. Eight generations deep, in fact, our family tree runs rich with the blood, sweat, and tears of those who have answered the call of the West Virginia woods.

So when they talk, he listens.

Once, when he was out there alone, his chainsaw halfway through the trunk of a tree, it kicked back hard when metal hit metal. And sure enough, there in the center of the tree was a horseshoe totally encased in wood that some old logger three generations back must have dropped down into the fork of a sapling when his horse threw a shoe. And there it remained until another logger, who had *also* started out using horses, found it a hundred years later.

Like I said, logging is just one of those traditions that hasn't changed much over time.

So you'd be smart to listen to those who came before.

Mostly when he's out there, though, it's the voice of his own dad he hears saying, "Boy, you better slow down, or you're going to get your dying done early."

And if there's anyone who would know about that, it was Grandpa Bill.

IN ALMOST EVERY PHOTO I've ever seen, Grandpa Bill stares back from the page wearing a white undershirt and a John Deere hat, with black-rimmed glasses that somehow always seem to make his dark eyes go darker. He always has this look on his face like he was in the middle of cracking some knee-slapper of a joke, but there are also thunderclouds behind his smile. The brewing, ominous rumble that at any moment the atmosphere might change.

William Eugene Bess Sr. was a second-generation coal miner turned logger, just like his dad before him, my great-grandpa Harry *Curl* Bess (his real name . . . you can't make that stuff up). If you were to pull up the West Virginia state flag right now, you would see two men—one with an ax, one with a pickax—both leaning against a rock in the middle. And so it was with my family: three living generations left choosing between two impossibly hard career paths. Between logging and mining. Between picking up an ax or a pickax. Knowing either way you lean, you'll find yourself between a rock and a hard life. And either way you go, it just might kill you.

Grandpa Bill loved fishing and hunting and camping. He also loved a round-faced pretty girl named Goldie, who he met one day when he walked into a diner where she was waitressing and swore right then and there that one day she would be his wife. They were married not long after in a courthouse ceremony, with only two witnesses and four black-and-white photos to prove it—the men in suits, the women wearing pillbox hats, and Goldie and Bill's hands resting proudly on the Bible.

Yes, Bill loved Goldie. He also loved red meat and smoked like a chimney.

And he dropped dead in the middle of the night from a heart attack before the age of forty-nine.

Goldie found him the next morning in the five o'clock darkness, when she got up to fill his lunch pail for work and tripped over his body.

Dad was already knocking at the back door so the two men who shared the same name and the same calling could ride in to work together. When he saw what had happened, he rushed in and grabbed his father up off the ground, rocked him back and forth in his giant arms, and sobbed silently as he buried his face against Grandpa Bill's.

"Oh God, he's already *cold*! He's gone, Mom, he's already gone, he's gone, he's gone!" A torrent of tears broke loose and flooded the kitchen floor.

All he could do then was whisper, "*Don't go, don't go, don't go.*"

And that's where everything starts to go into slow motion and begins colliding in my memory, as mine and my grandfather's stories intersect if only for a moment.

I was only two years old when Goldie found Grandpa Bill dead on the kitchen floor, so technically we had two years of crossover. But try as I might, the only living memory I have of my grandfather was on the morning that he died. Two is an awful young age to form your first memory, so I'll leave it up to you to decide whether these are my actual memories or just a series of pictures I have in my head from hearing other people recount it.

But I'll tell you right now, *it sure feels real to me.*

One. Goldie lets Dad in and one of them must have called Mom at the trailer next door.

Two. Mom is so in shock that she comes racing over and forgets to put me down first.

Three. We come flying in the back door and I see people huddled on the floor. Someone says the baby shouldn't be here, and then there are hands over my eyes and we're moving fast through the house.

Four. Some of the men who work for Dad and Grandpa Bill have started to arrive to ride into work together and are already knocking in the darkness at the front door.

Five. I'm being passed through the front screen door to one of them, and he's bouncing me and shushing me while I cry and cry despite his best efforts.

Count it out. This storm wasn't coming. *It was already on top of us.*

A porch light burns overhead.

I'm wrapped in something warm—maybe a red flannel work shirt—even though it is the beginning of July. The air is crisp and wet from a fog the night before, but you can already tell from the way it clings to your flushed cheeks that the day is setting up to be a scorcher. My sobs fade to quiet whimpers.

And somewhere inside, beyond a blazing porch light and the glass partition of a hurriedly slammed storm door, I can hear it.

A new widow wails in the darkness.

THE DAYS AFTER we found Grandpa Bill dead on the floor passed in a blur, but I'm sure at one point we buried him. Not because I remember it, but because I would visit that grave often with Goldie in the years to come.

My family sort of had this thing with taking a lot of pride in their own tombstones. They weren't always so much concerned about putting on a big show with the houses they lived in, but the graves they died in had to be top-notch. My grandparents, for example, had two vines full of roses engraved on either side of theirs. Over Goldie, there was a large bloom that represented her, a medium-sized one that represented Dad's sister, my aunt Lynn, and a tiny broken-off bud that represented the baby she'd lost in between. Over the freshly dug grave bearing the name Bill, there was a large bloom that represented him, a medium-sized one that represented Dad, and a tiny bud that represented me.

Like our own sort of royal rose bloodline.

Not to be outdone, Dad took great pains in designing the rock he would one day come to rest under, sending back multiple designs to the headstone company until he finally sat down and sketched it out himself. On it was a big log truck driving down a dirt country road (his favorite kind) and carrying a full load of trees. Beside that road was a stream, where a buck, a doe, and a fawn—Dad, Mom, and me—rested beside still waters. It wasn't clear at the time what happens in a deer family when the doe goes missing, but for the moment they were happy there, carved into eternity, resting in the unknown.

Not knowing what to do with themselves, Dad and the men who worked for him went back to work the very same day Grandpa Bill died.

After the ambulance had taken the body away with no sirens—there was no need to rush now—Dad had offered to send every last one of them home. But each man had stepped forward, hat in hand, and said, "We at least know the last thing Bill asked us to work on, and we'd like to stay now and do that work to honor him." And that's what they did.

There were neighbors on Fenwick Mountain who caught wind of that and didn't speak to Dad for months afterward, thinking it was just so disrespectful for him and those men to be out working when his own dad wasn't even in the ground yet.

But that's just the logger's way.

For a man like my grandpa Bill, who had spent his whole life working two jobs in the time it took most men to think about doing one, they knew there was no better tribute they could give him than to stay and work like he had: showing up even when you don't feel like it, working through the pain, and doing exactly what you said you'd do when you said you'd do it.

Days after the funeral—when they buried Bill in a brand-new suit that Dad had to try on first, stepping into a silhouette he never should have had to fill—Goldie would swear that she came home with an armful of groceries only to see my grandpa sitting there in his favorite chair, a two-year-old me in his lap. Most everyone in our family just chocked that up to the hallucinations of a grieving widow. Said that I had somehow just pulled myself up into the chair where she found me.

But I always liked her ghost-story version the best.

The following Monday came, and there were trees to cut and a team of men who would be counting on a paycheck come Friday, plus there was Goldie and Lynn to take care of now too. And so my dad—the crown prince of hard knocks and the heir apparent of Bess Logging Company—was tapped the would-be king.

And like the apparition of a handprint appearing on his back, he was once again marked for hard things. But unlike that nearly twelve-year-old version of him, this turn of events was not something he would have ever chosen.

This new job wasn't freedom. This job was loss.

Now you go to work. Your place is in the woods. Forget about the future. Forget about anything else you had planned.

This is your place now. Taking care of your family.

IT WAS CHRISTMAS EVE after the ghost of Bill had passed, and I was not yet three.

The trailer was dark, and I was the girl who couldn't sleep, so anxious waiting for morning to come. I crept out of bed, the wind whistling through the thin glass, aluminum-framed windowpanes, where a thick coating of ice had formed on the inside. I used my little hand to melt an opening to the outside world and saw a canvas of fresh snow on the ground below. It was the thick kind of snow that seems to fall all at once in one solid sheet, like a blanket laid upon a sleeping, sighing planet.

I peered through the glass, looking for any proof of the magic this night was supposed to hold, but saw only one lonely set of paw prints meandering their way through our yard—a small, tentative hesitation near our door, a hopeful pause in the direction of the promise of warmth—before giving up and moving on to the next yard beyond ours. That was all there was to see. Well, that and Goldie, up in the middle of the night and just walking around in her suddenly empty little red house.

Searching for an answer that would never come.

I crept through my bedroom and into the living room in only a nightgown—my lanky bare legs all shivering, and gooseflesh exposed to the icy cold. I held my breath and waited for the sound of the heat in the floor vents to kick on before cutting through the windows that connected the trailer to the lean-to addition. It was a maneuver I had done a thousand times before, and I knew just how to slip through without making a sound.

The house was sleeping and silent. The lights from the faux fir tree felt warm on my face, despite the cold cutting through the thin fabric line between winter and a girl who should have been sleeping. There were more packages underneath the tree than there had been when I went to sleep.

Something had changed in the middle of the night.

As I moved from present to present—shaking, listening, sizing them up—the crinkling paper must have cut through the silence and woken Dad from the middle of a deep, sound sleep. He sat straight up in bed, convinced someone was breaking in, and when he came to check on things, he didn't see me at first. When I stepped from the darkness into the light of the tree, it scared him so bad that he instantly went into fight without a thought of flight. He grabbed me with one strong hand and held me there suspended while he spanked me hard—*once*—with the other. My bare legs dangled and kicked at the air.

When he set me down with a thud, my feet barely hit the ground before they went running back to the safety of my bed. My backside was red-hot, with a single handprint already rising up. I was crying so hard, every other sob turned into a hiccup. I ran so fast I didn't even notice the blood running down the back of my legs.

But the blood wasn't mine.

A few weeks earlier, Dad had ripped the palm of his hand open on a saw while he was out in the woods learning to do something Grandpa Bill had always taken care of. And the wound had barely started to heal. When he spanked me in that fit of fear, the center of it opened up and started gushing red. But he was too scared to feel it.

Now in the retreat of his room, he looked down and saw blood on his hands. And he thought it was mine. It scared him so bad,

Mom had to spend the rest of the night going back and forth between our two rooms on either end of the trailer—the two extremes in our household—calming both of us down. Telling both of us over and over that we were okay, that it would be okay. That nothing permanent had been done.

But it *was* permanent.

Not the spanking, not the crying, not that Christmas night. But the new gaping wound in our family that had barely begun to heal from losing Grandpa Bill.

Something *had* changed in the middle of the night that year. By then our family had learned *everything* can change in just one night.

And looking back, now I know that being marked for hard things in our family wasn't just something limited to handprints of coal dust or dirt.

It was always something that ran in our *blood*.

6

something not always seen but felt

A YEAR AND A HALF LATER, when I turned four, Mom started cleaning houses again, just like she'd been doing when she first met Dad.

Except this time I went with her.

She and Goldie teamed up, and the three of us had our regular working rounds of paying customers. Mostly they were just other people's houses that we would go in and clean during the day while they were at work. But there were a couple of businesses—an office building and a beauty parlor—that we would go in and clean at night, when I got to stay up way past my bedtime in order to help out.

The beauty parlor was on Oakford Avenue, which cuts right down the center of Richwood, dividing the Main Street into an east and west and giving rise to the need for the only stoplight in town. It was in one of those connected storefronts, where it shared a wall with a diner on one side and a bar on the other. So you could eat, get your hair done, and drink away the woes of a bad haircut all in one stop, should the need arise. The decor inside was an exercise in 1950s modern, frozen in time, with its turquoise vinyl salon chairs, chrome fixtures, and black-and-white tile floor.

All of which reeked of perm solution and cigarettes.

We got right to work as soon as we unlocked the door. Mom wiped down the counters, Goldie swept all the hair off the floor, and I was given the task of washing the sink full of dishes in the back room by way of a tiny kitchenette. I can still remember those dishes, coated in the greasy red sauce of that afternoon's spaghetti lunch. I could just imagine the salon lady with her blue eye shadow, twirling pasta with a fork in one hand and an oversized spoon in the other while a single Marlboro hung from her frosted lips.

I can tell you this—at four years old, I was not the most diligent worker.

I just wanted it over with, wanted to go home already. So I devised a plan to cut corners anywhere I could, deciding to simply rinse, not wash, those dishes and get rid of any conspicuous remnants of the red sauce that way. But *dry* as I might, the slick of that grease remained. Its presence unseen but most definitely felt.

And Goldie wasn't having *any* of it.

"Mary Ellen, are you telling me you washed every one of these dishes with *soap?*"

She zeroed right in on that grease, knew exactly what I had done.

And my penance was to re-wash all of them by myself while Mom and Goldie waited. Even though the rest of the cleaning was already done and we could have easily gone home right then, they waited an entire extra hour while I re-washed every single one of those dishes properly. Alone. With the hottest water I could stand and elbow deep in dish soap.

As God had intended.

Goldie was the first one to teach me that a dish wasn't truly clean unless you were using water so hot it left your hands bright red. The scarlet red-letter way of knowing it was a job well done.

So there I was, four years old, up well past my bedtime, with bright red hands and up to my elbows in Joy. And it was the first of many times in my life that my family would teach me about work ethic and not quitting until a job was done right. About integrity and how it's something that is often not seen but *felt*. That it's about what you do when no one else is looking that matters. About starting over when it would be so much easier to quit.

That how you do anything is how you do everything.

And that in my family, we might not have had a lot.

But we *always* gave our all.

AS I GOT BIGGER, I inherited more and more jobs on Fenwick Mountain.

By the time I was five, it was my job to stack the truckloads of firewood Dad brought home from the log job. He stayed long after all the men who worked for him were gone and cut the extra wood to bring home to us. He wouldn't even think of cutting it while they were still there. That was company time. And company time meant getting as many logs as possible into the mill so those men could get paid. There were other families at stake. Other tables that needed food put on them. So only after they had given in to the exhaustion of the day did he stay on longer to take care of our own.

When he got home well after dark, you could see the truck laboring up the driveway, a great mountain of freshly cut wedges of poplar and birch and white oak loaded all the way up to the tailgate. And I already knew I would spend the entire next day stacking those pieces in our woodshed. That's how I spent my summers and early fall: getting ready for a winter that would surely come. When the wood was first cut like that, Dad always called it *green*, which mostly meant it was still wet inside and wouldn't burn. We had to cut and stack the wood during the warm months so it had time to cure and dry out if we wanted to have any chance at all of it producing heat come December.

It was a challenge made doubly hard by the conditions it was stored in.

The woodshed was a giant shanty of a building made from a motley crew of long-since-weathered boards that were never treated for the elements. It was ten feet tall and twice as long, with a single sloping roof that dropped down to six feet in the back. The only kind of roofing on it was long rolls of tar paper stapled directly into the wood. It still leaked, of course, but it more or less kept the firewood at least partly dry for part of the year.

Attached directly to the left side of the grayed-out woodshed was our much smaller, red-stained toolshed—stain that had been left over from Goldie's little red house—that held a single push lawn mower, some rusty rakes and shovels, plus a variety of smaller tools. And, on one particularly unfortunate Christmas, we had also housed every single one of our favorite ornaments—including all the ones from when I was a baby—out in that equally leaky toolshed. Come Thanksgiving, all we found was a soupy mix of cardboard, felt, and ruin. So Mom just went over to the store in town and put their display tree on layaway.

By January, we had a whole new set of memories.

My favorite part about the toolshed was that if I held the door open, I could step my way up the single-board shelves lining the wall and use the top of the door as the final push to hoist myself onto the roof of the creaky building. From there, it was an easy climb up in the back, where the slanted roof was lower, onto the neighboring woodshed, where I then raced to the highest front edge and ran a twenty-foot tightrope all along its full length.

Teetering on the edge of disaster and laughing at the ground ten feet below me the whole way.

On the far right side of the woodshed, the roofline disappeared into the uppermost branches of an old Red Delicious apple tree I always loved to climb, which in previous years had never been bothered to do the work of producing even one single piece of good fruit. In the winters, the bare-bone fingers of the branches scraped along the gritty tar paper roof of the woodshed, making the most awful screeching sound you've ever heard. It was like the lonesome wail of a white-haired woman dressed only in a nightgown of blowing, billowing snow—searching, always reaching, for something that was missing.

But the summer I turned six, that old tree surprised us all with a harvest so thick, it bowed the branches and littered the ground red with the most beautiful apples you've ever seen. Goldie couldn't keep up with all the apples I scooped up in my shirt and let tumble across her teal Formica kitchen table—the one with the chrome edging that she'd gotten when they first moved into the house in 1967 and never saw the need of replacing. So she took to boiling those apples down for canning, and for the next solid year we ate applesauce on everything.

Steak. Add applesauce. Pork chops. Add applesauce. Deer meat. Add applesauce.

Today I think they'd call that elevated, flavor-driven American fare. Goldie just called it necessity.

"People of necessity learn not to waste any unexpected bounty God sees fit to put in their way, Mary Ellen."

Apparently, hers was a version of God that was *also* quick to withhold good things. He doled them out in begrudging scraps, only to take them away again unexpectedly, at a cost made heavy over time.

And it was our job to just barely get by, to *survive*, until He saw fit to giveth again.

THE JOBS I STARTED to inherit on Fenwick Mountain were dangerous ones, indeed.

The wood had to be stacked just so—a row of upward-facing wedges followed by a row of downward-facing ones, all puzzle-pieced and different sizes like a giant game of Tetris, finding their perfect home. Otherwise the stack would become unstable and fall right over on you. I know this because it happened often.

In the pursuit of perfect stacking, I couldn't go a day without getting a finger caught, smashed between two pieces, until it was nothing to have at least one fingernail in the process of turning black-and-blue. When Dad unloaded the wood out of the back of the truck, flinging pieces into a pile on the ground, you had to learn to duck and cover at just the right moment or they'd hit you square in the belly and knock the wind right out of you. And more than once when we were out there stacking, I'd go to move a piece of wood only to find a fat, hissing snake underneath, irritated and telling me off for disrupting its afternoon nap. They were mostly just wood snakes, but once I found a rattler. After that, I learned to kick over the piece of wood first before I bent down to pick it up.

Sometimes when Dad brought home the firewood, he hadn't had time to chop it into pieces first. So he had me hold the huge stumps in place on the ground—my small hands covered in his giant, oversized work gloves that always smelled of saw grease and gasoline—and turn my face away for safety's sake while he revved the chainsaw and sliced them into pieces. The saw would be so close to my cheek that I could feel the heat off the rubber belt smoking as it turned its gritted teeth, chewing through the wood like it was half-melted butter. It would be so loud in my ears that they would ring out that *run-nun-nun-nun* sound for the rest of the night.

"Hold it by the edges," he'd say. "And if you feel it start to kick, you be sure and let go."

When blade met stump, a cannon of sawdust confetti, all earthy and wet and acid, filled the air and rained down on me like ticker tape. It filled my lungs with the thrill of teetering right there on the edge of disaster, walking a razor-thin tightrope between safety and that which would try to harm me. And when I escaped unscathed yet again, I'd spend the rest of the night picking those celebratory pieces out of my hair.

Once winter came, it was my job to tromp back and forth between our trailer and the woodshed every day—a distance of about thirty paces—hauling as many pieces of wood at once as my tiny arms could carry, which was usually only two or three. I'd put on my snow boots and a half-open winter coat and wade out into snow that was sometimes all the way up to my hips. Back and forth, back and forth, until the round firewood rack by the old wood stove was full.

And then I'd do it all over again the next day.

My job also entailed using a long wrought-iron poker to stoke the bright orange embers of the fire from the night before until it had enough air to throw another log on. Whenever I got to a particularly dry piece of wood, the kind that spontaneously combusted on contact with the coals, it shot flames straight up the charred stovepipe, and orange-and-blue blazes streaked out overhead where the metal wasn't properly fitted at the ceiling. It only lasted for a second or so, but it was enough to singe the drywall around the stove completely black four or five feet in every direction.

I don't know why, but it never occurred to us to fix it.

But of all the jobs I had that winter when I was six going on seven, the one I hated most was helping Dad off with his muddy work boots every night when he got home.

HE'D ALWAYS GET HOME well after dark.

Whenever I asked him just how much logging could get done once the sun went down, he'd always huff and shake his head at me.

"Kid, just exactly why do you think dozers *have* headlights?"

My dad wasn't a man of many words when it came to his work.

In the evenings, when he finally came through the back door that led inside the lean-to addition to our trailer, he was always encased in two inches thick of dried mud from the kneecaps down. It created a kind of loam cast, a terra-firma grip on his legs, where you couldn't tell where calf ended and boot began.

He'd sit down on our old orange-and-brown couch—a 1970s masterpiece consisting of large sprays of flowers inexplicably framing what looked like a painted barn scene in the middle of each cushion—which my parents surely must have inherited from Goldie when they bought that trailer and had no furniture and no money to their name. His jeans would immediately crease and crack like scorched earth, a web of lines splintering their way down his legs as large chunks of mud began falling away and aerially bombing the green linoleum below. By the time we were done, there would be more dirt than floor, and sweeping became an act of mere futility in those days for battling back that messy barrage.

I'd kneel down on the floor, my bare knees grinding into hard chunks of mud, and begin the process of breaking off the rest of it. Entire sections came off in my hands—like someone had taken a mold of what a hard day's work looked like—and I just cast them on the ground beside me. When I finally uncovered the laces to his boots, they were frozen solid. And as I tried to untangle them, my fingers turned the same bright red they always did when we stayed out too long sledding. They were crisscross laces held in place by metal teeth. And when I finally got them loosened up enough, I had to wrap both arms around a freezing, filthy, soaking-wet boot to gain enough traction to pull it off Dad's swollen, battered, bright red feet. When I was done, the only proof of my effort was one solitary mud boot imprint on my shirt, frozen there in fossilized time.

And then we'd do the other side.

I *hated* that job.

Truth be told, I resented it.

At the time, it felt like his way of giving me a horrible, lowly, muddy job just like he had. Of making me a part of this logger's existence he always said he didn't want for my life. Of having me bow down to the work that way, when he could have just as easily taken off his own boots and let me be.

Why did I have to have *his* dirt on my hands too?

It never even occurred to me that after twelve long hours of working, he might not have had anything left in him to take off his own boots. He left it all out in the woods.

But that certainly never stopped him from putting them on again each morning. Like that winter when they were logging on a particularly steep embankment and he jumped from the dozer just in time, breaking both his ankles in the process. When he came home that night, he said the doctor had wanted to put both of his legs in hard casts. But Dad knew that meant he would have to be out of work for six to eight weeks, which may as well have been a year for what it meant to us and the other ten families counting on him to keep going. The only thing he'd allow them to give him were a couple of air casts, because they were thin enough to still fit in his boots.

In my father's world, if you could get your boots on, you could live to fight another day.

FOR MONTHS, I got up an hour earlier than I needed to for school so that I could help Dad wedge those plastic casts and broken ankles into his still-wet work boots and get him off to the woods on time. We'd put those boots right up against the old wood stove every night, but they still never quite dried in time to go do it all over again the next morning. I think even they wondered, "What's the point in *drying*?"

I pushed and angled and shoved those brown leather vises up over his feet and fractured bones, and Dad winced with every movement. But in all the mornings we did this, I only ever heard him whimper once. Then I helped him up onto his two crutches and he was gone again. Out the back door and into the driving snow and whipping wind of the five o'clock darkness, lit only by a single sideways porch light knocked crooked some years earlier that had somehow never been set right.

I watched him like that for just a moment, kneeling from my place by that orange-and-brown couch. He was standing in the doorway, silhouetted against near whiteout conditions, the lone cast from the porch lighting up a million frantic, frenzied, darting pieces of flurry, like a snow globe someone had shaken violently and carelessly shattered to the ground. Broken, battered, limping on two crutches, he still looked larger than life to me.

It was as if the myth and the man had somehow just fused into one existence, solidified by the breaking of his bones. From that moment forward, whenever there was a man for three counties around who didn't feel like working, they would point to my dad, *already a legend in his own time*, and say, "If JR Bess can do it on crutches and two broken ankles, then who are you to stay home?"

In the rain, in the snow, in a full-on blizzard, he went out to cut the trees to build my future.

It was the kind of generational sacrifice that is not always seen but *felt*.

I THINK ABOUT that often.

I think about the boots and the bones, and how I didn't want to be so lowly as to stoop down and help another human being shake off their layers of mud. To wind up with their dirt on my hands.

I think that's because for a long time I believed freedom looked like getting to a place where none of the people were muddy. Where everyone was shiny and clean and took care of their own front yards. Where everywhere you looked, there were white picket fences and perfectly manicured pansies lining the front walkway. If freedom was a home, I think mine would look just like the house in *Father of the Bride*. It would be warm in the winter, cool in the summer, and have a mahogany wood banister I could slide down on my way to school. Afterward I would play basketball in the backyard in pristine new tennis shoes and then put on pearls for dinner.

People who wear pearls definitely do not stoop.

And then I think about God and what neighborhood He would live in.

I think about Jesus washing the feet of the disciples. Those dusty, busted-up, sandal-blistered feet they rolled up with to His supper table. I think about the Savior of the world kneeling there at His last meal, before His body was broken and His blood was poured out, first making sure that none of them had to walk around with muddy feet.

At this I picture Jesus kneeling at the feet of my father.

I think about the conversation those two might have. I think about the care Jesus would take in removing those heavy weights from around Dad's ankles. How He would hold all those broken parts in His light-filled hands and weep with Dad for all the pain he'd been walking around with. I think He would tell him that He sees how hard he's been fighting to hold it all together, sees all the sacrifices that he's made. I think Jesus would sit with him there for a while in the mud, not even caring about Dad's boots leaving marks all up and down His crisp, white robes.

There comes a time when every person who believes in God also has to decide what kind of character they believe He has.

Is He a cold and distant God, withholding every good thing, just waiting for the chance to take back what little He has given?

Is He a God who only gives out begrudging scraps of joy after first putting you in very hot water, His red-letter way of ensuring that you've been washed clean?

Does He keep you there, teetering on the edge of disaster and getting the wind knocked out of you over and over again, purely for His own entertainment?

Or is He a God who sits with you in the mud, who stoops to serve before the sacrifice?

I used to think freedom looked a lot like being around people who aren't muddy.

Now I realize we're *all* pretty muddy and maybe just a little bit broken too, no matter what kind of place we call home.

And when it comes right down to it, getting each other's mud on our hands—this serving one another in love—that's what true freedom has always been about anyway.

Because love, like integrity, is also about what we do when no one else is looking.

And how we do anything is how we do *everything*.

Mary
1988

7

these scars we bear

JUST AT THE EDGE of the field behind our trailer, where tall milkweed gave way to pines, there was a rusty wire fence intended to keep people out. But the obvious, gaping hole—created long before my time by someone who had pushed and stretched the protective boundaries from one side and then the other until there was an opening just big enough for an eight-year-old me to slip through—hinted at the fact that both the fencing and the Keep Out sign were there as more of a suggestion than a decree.

The woods behind our trailer dropped off sharply after that.

Plunging down and down, until sunlight soon disappeared behind a thick canopy of evergreens, the cool, musky-moss smell of the forest floor—thick and alive with a pulse all its own—filled the air and every corner of your lungs with dirt and earth and the feel of freedom. At times the path was more vertical limit than gradual decline, and you would have to cling from tree trunk to tree trunk, clawing your way down.

But at the bottom, breathless and alive, you would find yourself turned out on the first of many old, abandoned logging roads that crisscrossed their way down, cutting a path through the wilds like an underground city.

It was here that the real adventure began.

Sometimes there was a group of us—our own ragtag version of the *Goonies*—and sometimes it was just me. But I can tell you this, we were never back before dark.

Every road presented its own opportunity for inventing magic. Sometimes, like the true 1980s kids we were, we pretended like each twist of the road was another level in *Super Mario World*. And there were dragons to slay around every corner. Sometimes we didn't need imagination at all. The wide-eyed wonder of what was right in front of us was magic enough: a butterfly bush growing wild in the middle of a clearing, with thousands of blue wings that never seemed to land floating in slow motion on the breeze. Or a fallen log across a rushing waterfall that was never there before—created from the roar of a summer squall the day before—where we would tightrope walk across the outer precipice of danger without ever once a fear of falling. Sometimes we were in actual, real danger. Like the time we stepped right in a yellowjacket nest and went racing and screaming our way out of those woods. Each of us was stung no less than a hundred times, and one of us even landed in the hospital.

But you can bet we were right back out there the next day.

When we weren't in the woods, we were out on our bikes. Our merry band of misfits with skinned-up knees—hands in the air off the handlebars, seeing who could fly the fastest down the first steep hill—raced to a strip of old asphalt covered in a patchwork of grass that made up the airport at the end of Airport Road. When the days were especially long in the summer, we made that six-mile round trip no less than three times. Back home for only a minute, we would run inside long enough to grab a Dr Pepper and something to eat, and then we were off again.

And we *never* found our way back home before the darkness settled in.

The rules of my childhood were loose, fluid, and ever-changing. Generally speaking, they were to go out and play and not get into any trouble. There was the rule about being back by dark, but it was largely unenforced. More of a suggestion than a decree. Days could go by where my utter disregard for that rule would go utterly unnoticed. I could push it and stretch it like those gaps in the fence—slipping through the back door of the trailer well after dark and just in time for dinner—without so much as a cross word for six out of seven days in a row.

But on the *seventh* day, and without any kind of warning or explanation whatsoever about what made that day different from all the others, a storm cloud of sorts would come over Mom's eyes, and it was clear: everything *had* changed. She'd meet me at the edge of the gravel road as I slipped silhouetted through the darkness just now overtaking the dusk. I'd appear between the trees that divided our yard from the neighbors' next door, and she'd have me pick out my own birch switch. The same thin, recoiling branches my friends and I used as play swords, the ones that would make a *whhhhippp* sound when they sliced through the silence of the still, static air. Or she would just bring the belt. Either way, even in the blackness of the night, I could see the red welts raising up and down the backs of both my legs as we walked back home toward the trailer.

"Be glad you got me and not my mom," she would later tell me. "When she whipped us, if we'd been really bad, she would *braid* the branches first."

And it wasn't so much that I didn't think I deserved it. I just didn't understand what it was about this night that made me deserve it more than all the others.

The rules of my childhood were loose, fluid, and ever-changing.

And I got really good at seeing just how far I could stretch and push them beyond their limits.

I WAS A KID who liked to play with fire.

There was this thing that would happen among all the houses on our mountain. I call it *the bonfire effect*. One family would go out in their yard and throw some sticks and brush and old wood—maybe some garbage that had been accumulating for a little too long—in a big heaping pile right out front. They'd stack it all up, put it right there on top of the iridescent ashes still hot to the touch from the last time, still smoldering from the burn.

Then someone would pour gasoline on it and strike a match.

When that brush pile caught fire, it went up like a tinderbox. Shot flames ten feet high in the air. Acted like a beacon in the night. A combustible call to action for every family within ten houses who could see it, till one by one they came wandering into the yard. *Moths to a flame.*

When they came, they brought hot dogs and marshmallows, coleslaw and watermelon. Which we sliced in half, and everyone would grab a plastic fork and eat right out of the middle, red juices running down our chin without a care. Sometimes there was an entire cooler full of Icee popsicles, which were really just frozen sugar water. We neighborhood kids took turns sneaking them all night long when the parents weren't looking, till every last one of us was running wild all over the yard, seeing who could get closest to the fire without falling in.

Driven mad by the euphoric high of open flames and liquid sugar.

Inevitably someone brought fireworks, the serious kind that you're probably not supposed to have. And they'd go ahead and light them up too, right there, right beside the bonfire. Dad was always the ringleader in this. Sometimes he set them off from old glass Coke bottles. Sometimes he held them right there in his big bear hands and pointed them toward the stars like a rocket taking flight. *Dad wasn't afraid of anything.*

When those explosions lit up the sky, they rained down color on us in every direction. It reminds me of that scene in *The Sandlot* where there's one time a year, on the Fourth of July, when the boys can play a night game. Except for us this happened once or twice a week all summer long.

In a lot of ways, my childhood was a dream.

Some of those fireworks ended in these tiny little parachute men that came floating down from the firmament—they were always my favorite—and all us kids ran around picking them up, still hot to the touch, seeing who could collect the most. Then we'd poke marshmallow sticks right into the belly of the flames till they caught fire. We waved them around, leaving streaks in the darkness and seeing who could spell out their name the fastest.

Once, when no one was looking, one of us—*and I'm still not saying who*—went and stole a lukewarm Budweiser straight from the box that one of the neighbors had brought into the yard with them. And we split it, that *one* can, six or seven ways among us till we were all totally convinced we were drunk, stumbling and falling down on our backs in the grass to prove it, laughing from our bellies, and staring up at the stars exploding into supernovas in the dark skies above us.

Like I said, the rules of my childhood were loose, fluid, and ever-changing.

And I was a kid who liked to play with fire.

SKIN MELTS DOWN to tissue at 150 degrees Fahrenheit.

Mom and Dad were at work, I remember that. There was a baby-sitter, but by then she was passed out diagonally across their bed.

So I was more or less left to watch myself, only guarded over by an endless stream of movies on VHS. A motion-picture daycare adapted for the small screen.

Which was more than fine with me.

Another kid in the neighborhood had recently showed me how if you burn down bits of blue plastic until they are liquid, you can shape them into anything you want. Jewelry. Keychains. Doll accessories. Maybe I could even turn it into a business. Move out. Get my own place. The possibilities were endless. So I snuck a cigarette lighter out of the babysitter's bag.

And I set out to transform things.

With a flick of the thumb and a spark from the metallic wheel, a surge of butane vaporized into a white-hot flame. And a silently screaming piece of plastic turned sapphire jewel as it gave itself over to all the melting and dripping and bubbling. Sometimes transformation can be beautiful.

I didn't notice until it was too late how close the flame was creeping to my fingers. So in a panic, I just threw the whole thing—lighter and all—into the air. For a second, I couldn't find where the plastic had landed.

And then I felt the searing heat shoot up from my leg.

I smelled it before I saw it, the sickening scent of burnt flesh stinging at my eyes, and I started to gag. The pain was so white-hot that my brain couldn't keep up with where it was coming from. When I threw that plastic in the air, hot and melting, it tore into two pieces that both landed on top of my thigh—one large glob closer to the knee, and the other just a little higher up in the shape of a perfect V.

I didn't know what else to do, so I peeled them both off.

And with them came several layers of skin.

Leaving only iridescent ashes in their place. Still hot to the touch, still smoldering from the burn.

The place where the larger piece landed left an especially deep, gaping wound. It was so deep, it didn't bleed. I could run my finger along my thigh and feel it drop down into the white, pallid valley of my burn, and yet at the same time not feel a thing. Almost like that one spot on my leg had fallen asleep, but there weren't even pins and needles to wake it up. This was not skin, this was tissue. I felt like if it had gone one second longer, I would be staring at the full-red fiber of muscle.

Meanwhile, the V-shaped burn was really starting to scream. So I roused the babysitter from her quiet slumber and told her what had happened.

"You know, you could get into a lot of trouble for this," is all I remember her saying.

So just like that, we agreed.

Even though the temperatures were well in the nineties by then, I would spend the rest of that summer wearing long jeans to cover up those burns. So that *I* wouldn't get into trouble.

For weeks, it went on that way. My burns doing their best to heal over but constantly getting broken open from the friction and heat inside those jeans. Every time one would burst open, it sent chills down my spine, despite the dead heat of summer, as I felt those loose scabs open up once more, and a quivering middle—a hot lava of infection—would stick to the denim and run down my leg.

When I finally broke over and told someone, it was Goldie who took me to the clinic, where they confirmed I had one second-degree burn and one third-degree burn.

The scars of that summer, which I still have to this day.

SOME SCARS look like lightning bolts.

I once fell off my bike when I was little, a sort of head-over-handlebars situation that landed me on the gravel-covered ground.

Considering how hard I landed, I escaped relatively unscathed, and walked away with only one small gash across my right arm down near the wrist. A couple weeks later, after it healed over and revealed a shape strikingly similar to a lightning bolt (long before a young wizard made that cool), I reveled in showing off this new badge of honor and felt like the most untouchable kid in the neighborhood.

Some scars you don't mind showing the world.

Most scars, however, run much deeper than that.

SOME SCARS look like bruises.

I learned that one later in life when I couldn't quite bring myself to quit a boy who hit.

Still the girl who liked to play with fire.

It started the way these things always seem to. A lost temper here. A too-hard shove there. A pinned arm behind my back when he really wanted to make a point. Pretty soon, he would be sitting beside me and carrying on an entire conversation with someone else, just laughing right along, all the while pinching the backs of my arms so hard they would instantly turn black-and-blue, even through the cushion of my sweater.

I don't know if you've ever had someone pinch you hard on the back of your arm like that, grabbing hold of just the tiniest piece of skin and bearing down as hard as they can, but it's one of the most painful things I've ever felt. Not only for the actual injury it inflicts, but more so because it's a secret pain that can be kept hidden. Someone can be doing that to you right there out in public with everyone watching, and you just have to smile through gritted teeth. Because to react would be to make things far worse.

He could stop what I was saying, stop what I was doing, keep me sitting silent right beside him with one stealth move. And to the rest of the world, he looked like the most perfect boyfriend, always sitting with his arm around me.

Things took a turn for the far more serious when he started throwing me down on his bed, his hands squeezing hard on my face and throat, spitting his words all over me.

Shutupshutupshutup.

Once, when I moved to block him with a protective arm in front of my face, he grabbed my wrist tight with both hands and twisted violently in opposite directions until, staring at each other through wild, scared eyes, we both heard one loud *POP*.

My wrist still cracks to this day when I move it.

The final straw that nearly killed me was when he choked me hard with a chain around my neck. My brain was screaming at the lack of oxygen, burning at the edges like flash paper, the black ashes overtaking the light. I was down on my knees, praying through my last breath, when something snapped. The chain he was choking me with.

It was the necklace he had just given me for my birthday.

Afterward, he was sorry. Like he was always sorry. He cried and told me it would never happen again. But it always did. And I always went back. Walking hand in hand, his coat slung chivalrously over my shoulders, like the most perfect boyfriend.

Forever hiding the black and blue running up the back of my arms.

SOME SCARS look like a pressed-down place.

I learned that one earlier in life, when all I remember is warm, burnt-sienna light.

The July sun filtered through the dry, yellow-brown, overgrown field grass behind our trailer. These six-foot stalks—both aggressive and invasive in their nature, taking everything they wanted in their path—were topped by a plumage of gently swaying golden wheat. From a distance, you could even call it beautiful, this dance of theirs as if to music only they could hear. It was a summer psalm rustling out a wood-and-wind melody floating on the breeze.

But just beneath the surface was where both darkness and danger fell.

Just a few paces in, beyond the seemingly impenetrable outer wall of weeds that went well over my head, was a pressed-down place. A nest of stalks and flattened milkweed meets Queen Anne's lace that looked as if a large animal had circled and circled before finally lying down to die. When I lay in that same place, I thought about that animal. I wished I were that animal. Wondered what it would be like if I too could just decide to lie down and die.

As I lay on my back and waited for it to stop, I watched the bumblebees flitting above me, as if nothing in the world was wrong. As if anything in this world could ever be right again. As if a stranger, someone new to the mountain, hadn't just washed innocence away in driving sheets, like the rain from a hot summer storm.

I stared unblinking at the kaleidoscope of light coming in and out of focus through the wisps of wheat, casting warmth on parts of my body that should have remained unseen, a gently swaying Judas betraying me with its whispers and not shouts.

No sound of alarm.

No pending rescue.

No redemption would be found for me that day.

So, again and again, I let my mind go to another place. Far from that field. Far from that trailer. Far from where darkness hid in golden light. Away from the place where the protective boundaries had been pushed and stretched until there was an opening just big enough for me to slip through.

Far from the scars of that summer, which I still bear to this day.

8

leaving is a suitcase

MOM ALWAYS LIKED to tell me that we were from a long line of healers in her family.

When I was little, if I ever fell down or got scraped up or smashed my fingers in something, she would kneel down real close to my face, hold both my hands in hers, and tell me that we had the ability to heal ourselves. We just had to concentrate. Send all of our good energy to face our hurt. Show our pain just how big our power was.

You might think that was just to get me to quit crying, but she wasn't entirely making it up.

Once, when I got into an especially potent patch of poison ivy, I ended up with the entire left side of my face covered in painful, weeping welts. Mom went out into the weeds behind our house and picked touch-me-nots, milkweed, sumac bark, and some other stuff I'm still not sure of. And she brought it into our kitchen and mashed it all up into what she called a *poultice,* a homemade remedy.

This next part is hard to believe, but it's the absolute truth.

If you've ever gotten into poison ivy, you know that most of those welts take days, if not weeks, to fully heal. But Mom put that backyard mash on my face and told me to go lie down for a while. When I woke up just a couple hours later, those welts were totally gone without a mark left on me, as if it never happened.

If only all the marks life leaves on us disappeared so easily.

AT SOME POINT, Thomasina developed ear mites on one side that went untreated and caused the entire ear to shrivel and fold in on itself, making her look like quite the scrappy character. And scrappy she was. There wasn't a dog for ten yards that didn't fear her wrath, and I think she secretly reveled in her unchallenged domination of the entire neighborhood.

A year after that she disappeared.

She didn't get sick. She didn't get run over by a car. I just woke up one day and she was gone, never to be seen again. She was a good cat, and I loved her. I looked for her every day, hoping she would come back.

But she never did.

MOM AND DAD GOT MARRIED when she was just seventeen and Dad had not yet turned twenty-one.

Dad had actually proposed when Mom was sixteen. He went over to her house when she was home from school, sick in bed with the flu, and got down on one knee right there.

She said, "Oh, you don't want to look at me like this."

And he said, "I want to look at you for the rest of my life."

And that was that.

Because Mom was underage, her mom, a woman I would never meet named Zela Stanley-Booth-Duncan, had to sign a parental permission form. Four months shy of Mom's eighteenth birthday, that permission form was just days away from expiring. Zela told them she wouldn't sign another one if they let it run out, so they decided on a rush wedding at the local little Baptist church.

When I ask Mom why they couldn't just wait another four months, what the hurry was, she doesn't even think twice.

"We were in *love*."

"Yeah, but I mean, it was just four months. Would that really have changed anything?"

"It would have changed *everything*. I probably would have never gotten married."

That's because one month after Mom and Dad got married—and only one month after giving birth to Mom's baby sister—Zela died suddenly from a hardening of her heart.

If they had waited even one month longer, Mom would have dropped everything and moved away to go raise that baby.

I guess when it comes to love, timing is everything.

MOM WAS BORN Karen Sue Booth, the eldest of five kids from two different dads. Her own mom was one of six kids, including a trio of sisters whose names all began with the letter Z: Zela, Zena, and Zenetta. But it was Zela who braided the birch switches.

Mom was only sixteen when she came home from school one day and found a note from her mom that said, "You're old enough to decide for yourself now. The bills are paid through the end of the month. There's some food left in the cupboard."

Zela had packed up everything, including the other kids, and moved a county away to live with her new husband—the Duncan in Stanley-Booth-Duncan. She had offered to let Mom come with them, but Mom was just about to start her senior year of high school and felt that if she left, she would almost certainly drop out and never graduate. So she decided to stay. And with a paragraph of words in Zela's pretty handwriting, it bookended a legacy of leaving in Mom's already-broken family tree.

Her real dad left when Mom was only three, preferring the bottle to his family. I would meet John Booth (no relation that we know of to *Wilkes*) exactly two times in my life. The first time was when I was a little over a year old and Mom took me to meet him, where he promptly—in the middle of a bar, in the middle of the day—threw a screaming fit at her for daring to track him down. He yelled until she cried and told her he never wanted to see either of us again as salty streaks ran down her face.

It's funny, but I don't remember shedding a tear.

And then there was the second time, thirteen years later, when Mom took me to see him at the county jail where he'd landed a month earlier for DUI. When he came out of that hallway in his orange jumpsuit and sat down both a few inches and an entire world away from us, his glassy eyes seemed even more watery behind the clear panel that divided us. His cheeks were a purple-meets-red woven tapestry of broken capillaries that stitched out both a predilection and a pedigree for alcoholism. His own father had been a drunk. His brother was a drunk. *He* was a drunk. It was a family tradition.

This time, there was no sending us away. No yelling. No bar friends cheering him on. He had no one left. And so he desperately wanted us to stay.

But what do you say to a grandfather who is a total stranger?

We made small talk about me singing in the choir that year. The only thing in the world that he had ever truly loved was music and playing the guitar, and he liked to think that maybe I got that from him.

I don't want anything from you, played on repeat in my head.

I stared into his face, a face I had no reason in the world to remember, and found myself irritated by its familiarity. The eyes staring back at me—sunflowers surrounded by a field of green, green grass—were the same as Mom's. The very same ones she had passed on to me. The sideways turn at the end of our noses, the crooked little smile that always made us look just a bit sheepish. I stared into the familiar face of a stranger and thought, *There is nothing in me that will ever be like you.*

He was dead within the year.

So, *technically*, that was the third time I ever saw my grandfather. Laid out, looking respectable, glasses covering those sunflower eyes. A field of distance between the shouting, alcoholic haze of the man he once was and the shell of a man now quietly laid to rest. I didn't feel anything as I sat in that folding chair at the wake. No more than any other stranger would if they wandered in off the street, lured by the warm glow of lights and the promise of powdered creamer in the coffee.

I was sad for Mom, of course, who took it especially hard. She sat beside me and cried the real, honest, hardworking tears of a good daughter. A respectable showing for this respectable-looking, laid-out drunk of a man. But I felt nothing. I cried nothing. I showed nothing. At that point, I'd already learned how to slam the door of my heart shut to people who walk out of my life.

But all of that wouldn't happen for years to come.

WHEN MY SIXTEEN-YEAR-OLD MOTHER came home to a house with the electricity paid through the end of the month, there were a few boxes of shell macaroni and cans of stewed tomatoes in the cupboard. She lived on that for weeks, just boiled macaroni and chunky stewed tomatoes with a little bit of salt. A dish she still eats to this day. She started cleaning houses after school to make money, but it wasn't enough. When they finally turned the power off and she was going to have to come home to a dark house, Dad said she should just come live with him and Goldie and Grandpa Bill.

And, on an otherwise unremarkable gray day in March, just two months before her senior prom, Mom and Dad got married at a little Baptist church down the mountain. She wore Zela's veil, and Grandpa Bill bought her a plain white cotton dress that could double for her prom. Dad, with sideburns spilling all the way down to his jawline, wore a powder-blue tux. And the two of them to-gether looked so beautiful.

I know this because I've kept a photo taken in the church base-ment just after the ceremony. The two of them are standing together behind a three-tiered wedding cake from Donaldson's grocery store, letting those words "for better, for worse" hang in the air between them. It was a promise I believe they both meant. They just didn't know how quickly the "for worse" part was going to happen.

One month later, Zela was dead. It was a sudden hardening of the arteries, and one morning her heart just gave out. She was thirty-nine years old.

One month after that, Mom went to her senior prom alone because her new husband had already graduated, and school policy said he wasn't allowed to escort her.

After that, they lived with Goldie and Bill for another two years, until Mom was finally fed up. She told Dad she wanted them to have a place of their own, giving him both a deadline and an ulti-matum to make it happen. When the date came and went and he had done nothing about it, she packed up her bags and moved out. Two weeks later he came to get her, told her to come back home.

"*What* home?"

She spit the words in a way that made her top lip almost totally disappear, the way it only does when she gets really mad.

He told her, to the brand-new trailer that had just been delivered—*only temporarily and just for now*, just until they figured something else out—on the back half of Goldie and Bill's property.

Where it still sits to this day.

WHEN MOM WAS LITTLE, Zela rented a house down in Hol-comb, a small community on the outskirts of Richwood. If there had still been train tracks in town, that house surely would have been on the wrong side of them.

It had no running water, no indoor plumbing. And that left little Karen Sue Booth carrying buckets of water back and forth for her little brother and sisters, as she became the full-time, built-in babysitter. At the time, Zela was working at all hours down in Fenwick at the BF Goodrich plant, where she brought home a meager $200 a week to feed her and all her children.

At times they only had one pot of brown beans between them to last the whole week. Other times they made entire meals out of the welfare rice and commodity cheese the state gave them. At Christmastime, gift baskets mysteriously materialized on their front doorstep, though they all knew it was from a collection taken up by the people at church. That's the only way they could have Christmas dinner. And of course, if nothing else, there were always the oversized buckets of water that Mom would carry back and forth from the well, splashing as she went, so they would always be half empty by the time she got them to the house.

But my mom was always a bucket-half-full kind of person.

She was six years old before she got her first toy, a doll from the dump that her stepdad Jack found for her and cleaned up as a present. They had very few clothes, which were often dirty on account of no running water, and they were only allowed to get one pair of new shoes each year, just before school started. She gets really serious when she tells this next part.

"But we were *never* destitute."

I ask her, if that's not destitute, what exactly would be? What was this thin invisible line separating the two?

"We were *happy*." She says this last word like it's the most obvious thing in the world.

She tells me they may not have had toys, but they played stickball, made mud pies, went swimming, played hide-and-seek. She tells me how much she loved playing in the woods.

I ask her if she ever resented having to take care of the others and grow up so fast before her time.

"Maybe," she says. "But I also always admired watching my mom work so hard. How hard she struggled, but she always made a life for us. It's why I work so hard to try to give you things now. She always kept us together."

I ask her what she means by that last part.

"Well, at any moment she could have easily said, 'I don't want these kids.' Could have pawned us off on some relative. Could have split us all up."

I nod my head at this, even though it's not any kind of maternal bar of excellence I have ever considered before.

"But she didn't, she kept us together." She gets quiet here. "She always told me, *family stays together*."

THE MORNING she left is a suitcase.

It's open and it's full, then it's closed and it's gone.

I didn't find out Mom was leaving until the morning she left, when I saw her open bags there on her bedroom floor. She sat on the edge of her bed, filling empty containers with extra sweaters, dresses, and all the other baggage that had been building up for years. Everything in a lifetime that had contributed to her leaving. It all lay there, scattered around the floor in sorted piles. *What to take, what to leave.* And when I realized which pile I was in, a wound spontaneously opened up in my chest like a sinkhole so deep that I thought it would never heal.

The room filled with questions. Mine, not hers. *Where was she going? When would she be back? How did this all happen?* She was going on the road to work for a store called Ames, a new job full of promise and opportunity. It had come up quickly, unexpectedly, and she'd had to make a decision fast. As she explained all this to me quietly, calmly, I knelt down in a panic and started pulling sweaters out of her bags. Tried to turn the tides of her leaving. But she was already pulling away. The bags were so full now that the zippers bared their teeth in protest. The handles groaned under the weight of her decision. And I felt my own eyes start to overflow with tears.

She closed the door to the bedroom behind her. Quietly. Rationally. Without slamming. This was not an act of anger, it was an act of independence. She put the bags in the back of her car—an old maroon Oldsmobile that she would upgrade the first chance she got—and I watched the trunk latch without a sound. The trailer already felt emptier without her, and she was only in the yard. I stood in the doorway, hoping she would change her mind. Hoping she wouldn't be able to do it. But it was too late. The window for her staying had closed.

She crossed back through the yard, told me to give her a hug. And when I wouldn't let go, she pried my nine-year-old fingers from her coat and told me to be good. And I watched that maroon Oldsmobile drive away.

I stood in the yard a long time after her car disappeared, whispering through sobs, *"Don't go, don't go, don't go."*

But no one ever heard it. There was no one left to hear.

She was already gone.

WHEN A PARENT LEAVES, it just does something to a kid.

Or maybe I should say, it does *nothing* to a kid.

There was this movie I loved to watch when I was little, *The NeverEnding Story*, where basically this whole magical land called Fantasia is being destroyed by The Nothing. (Side note: If you've ever seen that movie and you're still not over what happened to Atreyu's horse in the Swamp of Sadness, I'm *with* you. Can we all just agree there should be a whole genre of therapy that is dedicated to 1980s kids who had their childhoods traumatized by that scene?)

In the movie, The Nothing is described as the emptiness that's left. A kind of despair destroying the world, sucking every good thing into it like this giant dust storm grown out of the utter *absence* of something. It's not even a hole, one of the main characters tells us, because a hole would at least be something. It's just . . . *nothing.*

It was kind of like that.

Everything just sort of twinged dark. There once was golden light and ethereal currents and gilded, glittered flecks.

And then there was nothing.

And I was no longer *safe, safe, safe.*

From a practical perspective, we know that kids who experience a parent leaving can go through everything from feelings of low self-esteem, believing they are unlovable, to having guilt that it was somehow their fault. They can wind up feeling abandoned and unworthy, experiencing confusion, grief, sadness, and shock at the suddenness of it all. They often have an unwillingness to form bonds or trust lest they get hurt again, difficulty expressing emotions, an unwillingness to show their true selves, and a deep, *deep* sense of shame that they somehow deserved it all.

And I suppose you could say that at one point or another, I have checked every box. But mostly when I look back on it now, I just remember the darkness.

The utter absence of something.

The emptiness that was left.

The despair expanding to every corner of my world.

Just . . . *nothing.*

Yeah. It was kind of like that.

9

none of it ever made her
feel more real

THERE ONCE WAS A BLUEPRINT who dreamed of being a real house.

Every day, she would draw and redraw her dimensions. She would change her oblong shapes into perfect circles, wishing that instead of a single sink it was still a his-and-hers vanity that took up residence in her happy home. She would close doors and open doors. Move walls that were still load-bearing. Layer on second and third floors to a ground level that was already shaky. A foundation that was crumbling under the weight of trying to become something she was never designed to be.

She would stare at her plans and wish for someone else's.

Something grander. More ornate.

She lost count of how many erasers she went through. Trying to undo the plain. Hoping to remove the ordinary. She would erase entire sections of who she once was, dust herself off, and begin again.

She became an expert in drawing straight lines, the ones that existed between where she was and where she wanted to be. She knew how to find relief in a staircase that was far too steep for most people to climb. She preferred walls to windows and never missed an opportunity to become more closed off.

She kept going until she looked good on paper.

But none of it ever made her feel more real.

WHEN MOM LEFT, she wasn't totally gone.

In the beginning, she would come back once or twice a month for a couple of days when she was off from work, and then it was once every other month, and then eventually it was just a few times a year. She was never *totally* gone. It wasn't like she walked out the door and I never saw her again. But all that meant was, *over and over*, I got familiar with her leaving. I lost count of how many times I watched her walk away. Lost count of how many times I watched the dust kick up in a fury under her fleeing tires—its hopeful, desperate display chasing after her down the driveway, arms always open wide . . . because it somehow never seemed to learn. I lost count of how many times I stood in doorways whispering, "*Don't go, don't go, don't go.*"

Until eventually I just stopped looking.

That's when I decided to stop focusing on roofs and to start building walls.

Over time, I've realized this thing I do when I think someone is about to leave me. Right then and there, I determine to become something so much *more*. I decide to go out and become so successful at something in life, to achieve something so great, that it will make them regret missing out on any of it. It makes me want to go out and do something so beautiful, so extraordinary with my one precious life, if for no other reason than it will make them sad that they weren't there to see it firsthand.

"That'll show them," I think to myself. "I bet then they'll wish they had stuck around."

The obvious problem with this plan, of course, is that it implicitly gives away my most deeply held fear and belief: *maybe they were right.*

Maybe without all this *more*, I was never someone worth staying for to begin with. Maybe they were right to leave. Maybe they could see right through me to all that was lacking. And maybe I will have to spend my entire life being more of something if I ever want the people I love to stay.

It's a pretty messed up way of getting even, if you think about it, this committing to tying yourself up in knots like that for the rest of your life just to prove someone else wrong.

Which inevitably brings me to the second obvious problem with this plan: if we are going to go out and create something beautiful and extraordinary with our lives, revenge is probably not the most fertile ground to start from.

It makes me think of a daisy growing wild in the middle of burnt, scorched earth—its thin, delicate petals wilting and withering in the heat, this beauty turning to ashes right in front of me at the hands of the very revenge-wasteland that grew it. Sure, we might go out and temporarily grow something pretty in the name of getting back at someone who wouldn't stay. From a distance it may even look like we're winning, this hope springs eternal in the midst of broken ground.

But the wilting, withering question remains: How long can we really survive that way?

THE SUMMER AFTER I TURNED TWELVE, we got one of those above-ground pools that comes in a big roll of hard plastic.

It was the kind where you're supposed to put stakes in the ground all around the outside and a blue vinyl liner on the inside. And then when you fill it all the way to the top with the garden hose, the pressure of it all—the water pushing outward in every direction, trying so hard to escape these artificial boundaries doing their best to contain it—that act of rebellion alone somehow helps the whole thing stand up. Mom got it on super clearance and brought it home with her one weekend. Someone had returned it to the store as defective because the vinyl liner had a small tear in it. But we just figured we'd keep filling it up with the hose, and that was that.

The water was *so* cold that first day we climbed in.

All the kids in the neighborhood came by to take a swim, and we were splashing around so much that the poor hose could barely keep up. But it didn't matter to me, because I could see a much bigger picture taking shape. We had a pool now. We had just taken in a stray black lab mix that was so pretty, she looked like she could be on the cover of a dog food bag. And Mom had just gotten a brand-new car. All the pieces were finally falling into place.

I hung my arms over the side of the plastic and talked to Dad as he stood on hard, dry ground.

"Well, Dad, what do you think? You've got a pool now, you've got a dog, there's a new car in the driveway. Wouldn't you say you're building a pretty good life? Do you feel like you've finally *arrived*?"

I shouted this last word, so he could hear me over all the splashing.

"Yeah . . . right. Arrived."

He seemed to almost spit the words, like he couldn't stand the taste of them. This bitter reality of how things just never seemed to get any easier, any better, no matter how hard he tried. He just kept shaking his head, muttering something under his breath.

I never got to hear what, though. Because a minute later, the liner tore loose and the hard exterior of the sidewall gave way. And a tidal wave of water went rushing under the trailer, dumping thousands of gallons and all us kids out on the grass in the process. And just like that, it was over.

This good life we were so close to building, gone in a *whoosh*.

COMPARISON IS A BOTTLE of dollar store vanilla perfume, a cheap cover-up, far too sickly sweet to be real.

I don't know at what age we first look up and start to wish for someone else's story. One minute we're playing peacefully in our rooms, blissfully unaware of the reflections all around us, and the next minute every mirror becomes an enemy.

I remember the first time I sat on the corner of my bed—face turned to the side, eyes straining as hard as they would go to the left, sizing up the bridge of my father's nose somehow planted and growing abundantly in the middle of my own face—just wishing so hard to lay claim to a different profile. A different kind of hard line to demarcate and delineate where his face ended and mine began. I would have given anything back then for one of those ski-slope noses, a tiny little run before the world's cutest jump. Instead I was left there staring, straining to see the whole mountain.

The summit of his nose to spite my face.

Those were the days when shame moved in and a deep insecurity began to take root. It coiled around my ankles—the scratching sound of dry scales on bare skin—a lying, hissing snake of a snare for my feet to get tripped up in again and again. When it wasn't forming shackles, it sat on my shoulders. This heavy weight that nearly broke my back as it bowed my head and lowered my eyes, a child now afraid to look up. It was a fork-tongued liar, whispering in my ear about everything in my life that I needed to cover up and hide.

For a while, I was the girl who got made fun of in school for my clothes. For how they looked and for how they smelled. So then I became the girl who sprayed on far too much dollar store vanilla perfume before I caught the bus every morning just to try and mask that scent of shame. Only it wasn't fooling anyone, a cheap cover-up that never seemed to work, far too sickly sweet to be real. I swear, to this day I can sometimes still smell that artificial saccharine combo of perfume meets mildew before I walk into a room.

It's the reason I hate the smell of vanilla to this day.

THAT FALL, as I started junior high down the hill in Richwood, I became best friends with a girl who it turned out lived not more than five miles—and yet somehow at the very same time an entire *world*—away from me.

Her family were all Baptists, which in reality is not all that different from the little Macedonia Methodist Church that I had always
gone to with Goldie. And yet, to take one look at the blessing that
was their lives, it would be easy to assume that God must have liked
them *way* better than us. Who knows, maybe it was because they
prayed harder, or maybe they always put more in the collection
plate. I don't know, maybe it was because Baptists dunked instead
of sprinkled.

Whatever it was, my twelve-year-old eyes started to see a distant,
indifferent God in place of the close friend I had always known.
This new God would go along and let this house be fine and that
house be fine, and then strike down the next one without any warning. It just seemed pretty obvious to me that He had His favorites.

And *we* clearly weren't it.

The first time I went over to spend the night at my new friend's
house, I felt like I was in some sort of 1990s sitcom—one where I
was the decidedly misfit sidekick. The Kimmy Gibbler in a world
where everyone wanted to be D.J. Tanner. It was the first time I
ever felt like a background character in my own life, a supporting
role to a story playing out right in front of my eyes—one that to
me clearly seemed much better than my own.

My friend's family lived one mountain over, in a two-story house
that was always immaculately cared for. Rather than aluminum
and mismatched wood like we had, they had pretty vinyl siding
and a real brick foundation. Out back they had an in-ground pool
surrounded on all sides by a custom two-level deck that they built
by hand themselves. Their version of the good life clearly wasn't
going to get knocked over at the slightest push.

They drove a pristine white Buick that we were never allowed to
eat or drink anything in, so it still had that new-car smell years after
they bought it. They had one very fluffy little dog that looked like
it got bathed every week. It slept inside at the foot of my friend's
bed and was in every one of their carefully coordinated Christmas
photos. It was the first time I ever realized that keeping your dogs

chained up outside year-round might not be the norm. My friend's family seemed to have built a life that was everything they ever wanted.

And I was quickly realizing that it was everything *I* could ever want too.

In so many ways, their family became the example in my life of *what could be* and *what the good life looked like* at a time when all I could focus on was what had been lost. I spent a lot of nights hanging out at their house, and they took me in and became a second family to me. Looking back on it now, I realize they taught me more than I'll ever be able to thank them for.

They did a lot of things differently than we did. They were savers. They didn't go into debt to buy things only to have the bank take them back later. Instead, they only bought what they could afford and paid cash so they never paid any interest. They then turned around and used that money they saved and invested it. They made their money go to work for them, and they always somehow seemed to have enough.

They sat down at the table together for dinner every night. They held hands and prayed before eating. They spent their weekends doing house projects or working in the yard, caring for and taking pride in the things they had so they would last longer. They did things ahead of time, like ordering Christmas presents, and used a fund they had saved all year just for that. Their house was always warm and clean, and I learned from them that you can't dry your white clothes in the dryer or they'll turn yellow. I know that sounds silly and simple, but those were the kinds of things I just never had someone around to tell me before.

My world was in a tumble, a free fall. And being around them felt like landing on sure, solid ground.

In those days, I became even more obsessed with somehow transforming our brown single-wide trailer overnight into a real house just like they had. I'd spend every afternoon and all weekend cleaning it. I tied bows around all the curtains that I made out of tiny scraps of mismatched fabric. I took down the flypaper strips that were dotted entirely black with a hundred little fly corpses. Broken bodies that were once born to fly but instead perished right there, stuck in the glue that bound them. I burned incense, but it only made the place smell worse. I dumped an entire bottle of shampoo and two full buckets of water directly on the carpet. On my hands and knees I scrubbed, my bare fingers digging in to the dry crusted places where the cat had gone and plucking mushrooms that were growing right out of the fibers, my hair getting soaked by the filthy water. But none of it changed anything.

Every day, I would draw and redraw blueprints of the dream life I one day wanted to build, these hard lines of a profile I wanted so desperately to change. And when I flip back through the plans in my mind, now I see it.

It was always my friend's house that I drew.

By the time I was fifteen, I had started going with them to church every Sunday.

The Baptist preacher at the front had jet-black hair that reminded me of the jagged pieces of coal Goldie kept heaped in a big wooden corral on the far left side of her back porch and sparsed out in half-full buckets all winter long. He seemed to me more city-slicker car salesman than backwoods country pastor.

He was a fire-and-brimstone kind of preacher, and when he really got going, both his cheeks flushed blood red, while the rest of him stayed decidedly gray. When he decided to hold a revival week, it seemed to me a performance so full of huff and bluster that it just might raise the rafters and rattle the roof. He shouted Scriptures, pounded the pulpit with balled-up, perfectly manicured fists, paced and raised his hands high over his head till his double-breasted jacket couldn't stretch any further, and then shouted some more.

I had never seen anything like it.

Monday turned into Tuesday turned into the rest of that first revival week. And each night I went with them. I sat in the back of the church and listened closely, at first with amusement and then with increasing interest. There was something stirring in my heart that I had never felt before. It took hold of me in a way that wouldn't let go, and by Friday, I found myself walking up the red carpet to give my life over to God. Not *because* of the red-faced, blustering preacher at the front of the aisle—just to be clear—but *despite* him. Which just goes to show, when God is ready to take hold of your heart again, He's going to find a way to reach you.

No matter how unlikely the messenger.

A few months later, I was baptized in the big tank at the back of the altar, just behind where the choir stood. Goldie came in her best Sunday-morning, pink church-lady suit, even though it was just a regular old Wednesday night. And my friend's mom cried at the piano as she played *Amazing grace, how sweet the sound.*

When I emerged from that water, a former wretch like me dripping wet in a T-shirt and shorts, it felt as though I was being born into a new life. Not just a life with God in it again, but a life where I could be more Baptist than Bess. One where I was finally washed clean and acceptable in their world. If God was picking favorites, I wanted to be on His team.

Bring on the blessing, God. I'm more than ready.

But I would later find out, when I took my baptism certificate home, that this was none other than the same little Baptist church where Mom had gone herself when she was a teenager. The same little Baptist church that she and Dad had gotten married in. The same church basement where they shared a grocery-store wedding cake. My family already had plenty of history in that church, and so far it hadn't changed anything.

I thought I was going there to get a different story.

But it turns out, the past just has a way of repeating itself.

the scars that stitch us back together again

THE TOWN OF RICHWOOD begins as you top over the last hill just after the Cherry River snakes lazily to the right, parting ways if only for the moment from its asphalt companion, destined for a more meandering path. Somewhere around the time you let off the gas to coast the rest of the way down, Highway 39 officially turns into Main Street, and not far off in the distance you can see a faded rainbow pennant garland crisscrossing from telephone pole to telephone pole and heralding in your arrival.

The whole town has a wash of Kodachrome to it, like a postcard from the 1960s where the once-vibrant color has begun to fade, only adding to its charm. The mishmash of brick buildings are painted all different shades of red and orange and yellow and brown, matching the sun-washed kaleidoscope triangles of the pennants waving overhead. And the double yellow line down the center of the road leads the way, ever onward, to the pot of *once-was-gold* at the end of the rainbow, in the form of the old sawmill.

Come August, the blazing orange-and-black band uniforms of the Lumberjack Express will be the most vibrant thing in town. The Lumberjack Ladies will execute a precision twirling routine—the same tradition they've been carrying on since Dad was in high school there—and the bass line will thud out a drumbeat of pride that swells in the heart of every onlooker who has ever been lucky enough to call Richwood home.

Like so many small towns in West Virginia that only came to exist orbiting around the new mill or mine that had become its very epicenter, Richwood was established when the Cherry River Boom and Lumber Company began mill operations in the small valley at the base of a mountain chain they determined was "rich in wood." *Rich. Wood.* And the name stuck.

At the time of its founding in 1901, Richwood recorded only twenty-four inhabitants. But by 1922 that number had grown to over seven thousand in less than a quarter century, thus putting the "boom" town in Cherry River Boom and Lumber Company. Once Richwood was a town that glittered with promise and possibility. New businesses opened and flooded Main Street with clothing stores and furniture stores and restaurants. But in 1924 the Boom Company was ravaged by a fire. They rebuilt, but as the years wore on and the timber industry took harder and harder hits, the mill and the surrounding businesses struggled and went under, including the tannery, the hub factory, the paper mill, and the world's largest clothespin factory, all of which had once called Richwood home.

Eventually, a different mill went in, and then another after that.

But for Dad it was never the same. He saw the way of life that he'd been raised on quickly disappearing. And by my senior year of high school, he had never felt that more.

It felt like everything he ever loved was leaving.

SOME MYTHS are much closer to fact than fiction.

There are some heroes who shrink in the shadow of the legend they cast, this illusion of a man made much larger than life, but only through the projection and protection of the outer veil of curtains they are so quick to hide behind. This sleight of hand and magic misdirection that somehow takes snake oil salesmen and turns them overnight into the great and powerful Oz. Just pay no attention to the mere mortal you see cowering before you in the corner.

There are some tall tales who only ever get that way by first standing upon the shoulders of the giants who came before them. They will crawl right up other people's backbones if they have to, using every vertebra as a stepping stone, willing to walk all over everyone so long as they come out on top. And sure, the view may be nice from up there. But make no mistake, the merits of that particular kind of character are *highly* exaggerated.

And then there are those heroes who just always had an origin story worth believing in. That's the kind of man-fused-with-myth my dad always was. A legend living in his own time. And if anything, the stories of his daring exploits have gone largely underreported for far too long.

This, after all, was the man who was called on to chop down a 150-foot water tower—a sawmill relic of better days gone by, that stood blistered and rusted in the heat of the summer sun—with nothing but a welding torch. As the whole town gathered round, Dad set about bringing that giant down.

When the first leg was almost cut through, that old tank started creaking and moaning in protest, and entire bolts still fully intact started shooting out of the ground like four-inch-wide bullets. As that tower started down with a heavy sigh, the other three legs came straight out of the ground, just like someone had picked up a toy and turned it over. But at the last minute, it caught on that first notched leg that Dad hadn't cut quite short enough. There it stood suspended in midair, leaning at a forty-five degree angle.

A rusty, roaring, red oak refusing to be brought down.

He kept cutting, and when it finally hit the ground, that tower sent a cloud of rust so high in the air you could see it from a mile away. But when the dust settled and the air cleared, it had landed exactly where he intended, as if he had marked an X on the spot. Everyone in town thought it was so professional how he brought it down nice and slow like that by notching that first leg just right. And the next day, there it was on the front cover of the newspaper. Dad standing next to that downed Goliath of a tower looking like David himself.

Good news travels fast in a small town.

This was also the man who, when every other logging company for three counties around said it couldn't be done, was brought in to log "rattlesnake country"—a beautiful tract of timber way up in South Fork that was absolutely eaten up with timber rattlers crawling out of every and all directions. His crew saw no less than thirty-four that summer, and they quickly learned there was truth to the old legend that a dead rattlesnake will still strike at you until the sun goes down. Perhaps the closest he came to disaster was when he was cutting down a tree and noticed that the pile of sawdust below him was moving. It was a rattlesnake that had been between his feet the whole time.

When I asked him what he did, he didn't even have to think about it.

"I just kept right on cutting. I didn't want to be the one to bust up that beautiful tree."

This was the man who once pulled a cement truck out of the Cherry River after it lost control and came skidding down Fenwick Mountain so fast you would have thought its brakes were on fire. What a whole team of wreckers wasn't able to do in two weeks, JR Bess got done in a matter of minutes, just him and his trusty dozer. Even when that steed sat straight up on its hind blades with him inside, bucking under the weight of that which would try to drown him, he rode that yellow beast back up the river bank, pulling the cement truck behind him to safety.

This was the man who tied himself with ropes to a sheer cliff and kept on logging when everyone else said it was far too steep to climb.

This was the man who had a black bear wheel around and get ready to charge him, and—not knowing what else to do—just growled right back at it until that bear took off running.

This was the man who was struck by lightning and it somehow only made him stronger.

And *this* was the only man the governor could call on to cut the tallest, straightest, strongest trees in the entire state of West Virginia to replace the historic bridge at Philippi the year it burned down.

For miles around, people would point to my Dad and say, "There goes the legend. That old boy is West Virginia logging royalty." And they made it official when they named him the 1990 West Virginia Logger of the Year.

But there's a problem when you live with a legend.

You can never be sure he's going to make it back home.

IT DOESN'T TAKE a very big tree to kill you.

Dad learned that the hard way when he was still in high school. By then he had taken to going half-days to school so that he could spend his afternoons and evenings in the woods. He'd walk to the still-booming sawmill on the other side of town and hitch a ride with someone who was driving up into the woods. There were always plenty of people working in those days.

On this particular day, he was up at the landing by himself, running the loader to get another truck full of logs out to the mill before sundown. And that's when a small birch sapling came right down on top of him and split his head wide open. He had to climb off the loader and drive himself back to the mill, stopping every few feet to wipe the blood out of his eyes. By the time they got him to the hospital, doctors said he was lucky he didn't die out there alone.

There's a reason dead branches are called "widow-makers," and one of the first things a logger is ever taught to do is look up at the danger always hanging over their head. When those branches take a bad hop, they'll shoot right back at you like the bullet out of a gun. Once, when Dad took one square to the chest, it hit with enough blunt force to break the bone, and the doctor said he had no idea how it didn't stop his heart right then. He said he should have died right there on the spot.

There were a lot of times like that when Dad probably *should* have died out there in the woods, but he didn't. This is, after all, no mere mortal we're dealing with.

There was the time he caught a chainsaw to the hand and had to be rushed to Morgantown to save his thumb. There was the time a dozer rolled over with him still inside. There was the time a piece of equipment kicked back and split his forehead wide open right down to the bone. And we've lost count of how many times he's had branches come down on him. And it didn't just happen to Dad.

Once, one of the men who worked for him came down off the hill holding a work glove to his mouth. The bright, warm sun coming through the trees cast a shadow of a doubt from the man's hardhat across his face, so Dad couldn't see anything wrong until he was right up on him. But then the light moved just right and he saw something he would never be able to unsee. A rogue branch had caught a bad hop to the side of the man's nose. *And it had taken off half his face.*

They medevacked him down to the big state hospital in Charleston where they were able to stitch him back together again. Eventually, he even returned to work. Because that's just the logger's way. But I can tell you, Dad didn't sleep through the night for a month after that.

Like I said, it doesn't take a very big tree to kill you.

But luckily Dad was always somehow bigger.

WHEN I WAS LITTLE, Dad took me with him to the woods.

He'd let me sit on his lap and pull the levers to run the dozer. My feet, of course, couldn't reach the pedals, so he'd have to do that part. But I could steer it left or right and make it climb high up on the hill. Or if I really wanted to have fun, he'd let me just hold down one of those levers and the dozer would sit there spinning in a 360 like a big yellow merry-go-round. I thought it was the funniest thing. When we weren't doing that, he'd let me sit in the claws of the loader and take me high in the air like it was the world's biggest swing. It got grease stains all up and down my jeans, but I didn't care.

When I was *really* little and wasn't supposed to be there, he and Mom would hide me away in the sleeper cab of the Kenworth big rig, a striped yellow, orange, and brown 1980s eighteen-wheeled dream. And when I got older, he showed me how to use a chainsaw and even let me cut down my own tree. But most of the time when I was up there in the woods, I would run wild, climbing through the treetops of the giants he had just taken down and wondering how life could ever get any better than that.

I wish you could've known Dad back then.

He was so young and handsome and full of life. He loved to laugh, and he was always pulling pranks on the men who worked for him. A big old bullfrog in somebody's lunch box. Chainsaw grease in somebody else's sandwich. When he really got to laughing, his whole body shook until it didn't make a sound anymore and tears just rolled down his face. Dad didn't *always* have the weight of the world on his shoulders. When he got home from work, I'd crawl through the window connecting the trailer and the lean-to addition and sit on the back of the couch while we watched TV together. We were inseparable in those days. The best of friends.

Nothing could ever tear us apart.

BY THE TIME I was finishing up high school, Dad and I started to have ourselves an earnest battle of the wills.

He'd come home wet and exhausted at night, sick and tired of being covered in mud, sick and tired of being cold and soaked to the bone, sick and tired of *being sick and tired,* and in no mood for hassle. Years before, at Grandpa Bill's funeral, Dad had overheard two men talking about how the logging business would surely go under within a few months now that he was in charge, and he had spent every waking day since then—knee-deep in the mud and struggle of his own revenge wasteland—tying himself up in knots just to prove someone else wrong.

And when he came home, he was met by his mirror reflection. Every single similarity in us that drove us to our differences.

Mouthing off was like my new favorite hobby in those days. And I was *good* at it. I was good at the eye roll. Good at firing off the low blow. Great, even, at the huff-and-stomp-off. But perhaps my best talent of all was letting Dad know daily just exactly what an eternal disappointment it was for me to live in that trailer with all its filth and stink and leaky, falling-down ceilings. We got into each other's faces a lot that year.

But never so much as the night with the refrigerator.

A few years earlier, I had taken to collecting magnets of all the states I'd visited—I was up to thirteen at that point—and arranging them on the freezer door like a map of possibilities spreading outward from my West Virginia epicenter. We had gotten into it over something that night, and the next thing I knew those magnets were pressing hard into my back, cold and uninviting, as we shouted at one another. He yelled so close to my face that I could feel the heat of his breath, could smell the Dr Pepper, while he poked me in the chest with one chainsaw-grease-covered finger.

"Kid, by God, if I tell you to do something, then you better DO it!" He thrummed out each word in a steady drumbeat over my heart while Ohio dug ever deeper into my shoulder blade.

I had always been afraid of making Dad mad before this. It used to be that all he had to do was huff a sigh in my general direction and I would immediately straighten up from whatever it was I'd been doing. But there was something different rising up in me now. His sighs had no power over me anymore.

It was like a rebellion was breaking loose in my backbone, over-throwing everything I didn't want my life to be. A switch flipped in me, and we weren't going back. In that moment, with him just inches away, red-faced and hollering through gritted teeth about everything I better get my act together on, I set my jaw and defiantly raised my chin just a little closer to his. I stiffened my spine—like a steel lightning rod where mere vertebrae used to be—and felt my chest spread open to meet his. His work boots were going toe to toe with my bare feet, cold and muddy against my skin. He towered over me. I was pinned between a refrigerator and a man the size of one, with the never-ending spread of his shoulders blocking my exit on either side.

But I wasn't running.

I narrowed my eyes to bare slits and glared at him, unblinking, contempt and disdain shooting out of them like concentrated laser beams. Even when he got louder, I refused to flinch. That was the moment we both knew.

It was time to put away childish things.

I SPENT A LOT of time in my room in those days.

When I saw those truck lights pull up, always well after dark, I'd head for my neutral corner of the trailer and slam the door shut. Once, I even packed up all my worldly belongings and moved next door to live with Goldie. But that didn't last long when she actually wanted to tell me what to do—when to go to bed, when to do my homework. I'd been looking out for myself far too long for someone to try and tell me what to do now. So I packed up my things and stomped the fifty-some paces back across the yard, trudging through the snow and resigning myself to that trailer. And the door-slamming started all over again.

That was the state of our standoff when Dad came home one day with his hand wrapped in a Bess Logging sweatshirt. The year he'd won Logger of the Year, Goldie had them made over at the Sheltered Workshop, the place in town where they would screen print your latest accomplishments on any number of things. We tend to do that, don't we?

Wrap up our wounds with our latest accomplishments.

DAD HAD CHOSEN A BEAVER as the Bess Logging Company mascot. He named it Bucky Beaver, and it was a Sasquatch of a thing with overalls, a hard hat, and razor-sharp buck teeth. The year he won Logger of the Year and was also honored in the Cherry River Festival as the grand marshal of the parade, he actually had the thing turned into a full-fledged costume with a giant papier-mâché head and mesh wire for the eyes. And the six-foot-tall, full-grown men who worked for him all took turns wearing it. It looked like Sasquatch had officially come down from the mountain to terrorize all the townspeople in the form of some radioactive super-rodent.

Which Goldie subsequently had printed on those sweatshirts.

I got to ride in that parade on the back of a pickup truck with an embarrassingly oversized sign that read "Daughter of the 1990 West Virginia Logger of the Year" and throw tiny Tootsie Rolls at all the little kids lining Main Street. Dad was ahead of me, riding with the T-Tops down on a red Camaro, leading the parade.

He looked like royalty or a hero coming back from war, riding down the middle of town that day. I remember how he seemed to move in slow motion, waving and smiling to the crowds of people shouting out his name. It was as if ticker tape rained down on him from the rainbow pennants waving overhead in the August breeze. And the whole thing played out right before my eyes like some sort of Super 8 film, with all its blips and pops and camera reel skips. The instant nostalgia kind of rewind that seems to say, *Whatever you do, don't miss this.*

And right then, right there, in that moment in the back of a silver Chevy pickup truck with the title "daughter of" hanging over my head, I think I already knew.

In the future, when I looked back on my Dad . . . I wanted to remember him just like this.

WHEN WE UNWRAPPED that sweatshirt from his hand, blood had seeped in and coated the entire screen printing, making it look like Bucky Beaver had mouthed off to the wrong person. There on Dad's right hand—middle finger, middle knuckle—I saw the source of the bloodbath. Apparently, he got his hand too close to the ax blade sharpener, a round piece of grit spinning like a sander, and in a split second it took off the entire hide of his finger almost down to the bone.

In true JR Bess fashion, he just rubbed some dirt and chainsaw grease on it and kept working. And now, eight hours later, it was my job to try to clean it out. We sat together on the couch—me with a bottle of peroxide and him with that washed-out gray color his eyes would get when I knew he was really sick or hurting something awful—and I began to reopen new wounds.

He flinched with each swipe of the Q-tip, but he never asked me to stop. It took over an hour, but I finally got it all cleaned out. And all I knew to do after that was to put Neosporin and some gauze on it, held in place by a few large Band-Aids. I told him we should get a doctor to look at it. But he just said "Ohhh, it'll be alright" and "I'm tough, I can take it" in that way he had, where you couldn't tell if he was more stubborn or tough or scared, or some combination of all three.

And that was that. For the next six weeks, I tended his wounds. Every night he came home and I spent a good hour with him, cleaning and re-dressing the injury. And every day he went back to work and got it dirty all over again.

It was a long road back. It took a long time to heal.

There were setbacks and infections along the way. But slowly, day by day, I watched as that wound stitched itself back together again. As the gaping divide got smaller. And every night we spent together, talking about our day while I performed nothing short of minor surgery with tweezers and a cotton swab, it started to grow us back together again too. Day by day, the gaping divide between father and daughter got smaller.

It took me a while to realize this in life, but sometimes these wounds we bear serve to slow us down long enough so we can really start to see each other again. To bring healing. To open us up so we can flush out the poison that has started to take root in our lives. I'm not sure what would have happened between my Dad and me if he hadn't torn his hand up that day. We'd probably still be slamming doors.

Instead, we learned what it looks like to heal. *Together*. And when that wound finally closed over—hand to God, you can't make this stuff up—the scar that remained was in the shape of an M.

Which I just took as a sign that we belonged together.

We always joked that I left my mark on him with that M. But the truth is, that was the kind of healing that left its mark on both of us.

Thank God for these different kinds of scars we bear.

The ones that stitch us back together again.

My mind goes back to a Christmas when I was five, maybe six. Dad loaded me in the pickup truck with him and made sure my seatbelt was fastened tight. My feet didn't touch the floorboard, so I swung them back and forth and looked down at my snow boots with the red laces and the metal teeth running up the length. Size small.

I stared out at a pale blue blanket of snow as the first stars of Christmas Eve blinked in and out of existence. Dad started the engine, and the grease still covering his hands left smudges on the steering wheel. He turned up the heat and pointed his vent toward me, and as we drove away down the driveway, big clumps of mud still stuck to the tires from him going to work that day fell off and left tracks in the snow.

In case we needed help finding our way home.

He drove us to the store and parked near the door, tailgate first. We went in, and he held my hand while he talked to people much taller than me. They tried to help him, but he already knew exactly what he wanted. Ten burnished brown cherry gun cabinets, with the etching on the glass and the curio display. To go, please. The man behind the counter had to pick his jaw up off the cash register before he could ring him out, and the whole store stopped to watch as they loaded those cherry cabinets in the back of a muddy pickup truck.

He fastened my seatbelt tight again, and we spent the rest of the night driving to ten different houses with ten different sets of Christmas lights, the homes of the ten winter-worn and weary loggers who worked for him. We knocked on doors and gave fruit baskets to the wives and brown teddy bears with red-and-green scarves to the kids. And then I watched him help unload each cabinet and stand in the doorway of those ten homes as he thanked the men in front of their families. Thanked them for putting it all out on the line, for being his own band of brothers. For working from sunup to sundown, day in and day out. Even when they were hurt, even when they were sick, even when it was freezing outside. He told them it was a job they should be proud of, and he told them how proud of them he was.

And all the while he was doing this, I wasn't watching their faces. I wasn't even watching his. I was watching the faces of their kids. At how they stood a little taller. Looked at their dads a little differently. How they felt that pride inside of them too.

I was five, maybe six, and even I knew that he had probably spent his very last dollar buying those cabinets. But that night I also knew that it didn't matter, because we were the richest people on the planet.

That was the night Dad taught me what it really means to build someone up, to be grateful and humble and say the things that need to be said. To make room at the table for everyone, and to maybe work a little miracle somewhere in there too.

Sometimes it's easy to get lost in this old world and forget what really matters. But then I remember nights like that, and I'm grateful that I'll always have his example to remind me.

In case I need help finding my way home.

interlude

IN THE FLICKERING, green, beeping darkness, my faithful words failed me.

They ran and hid in corners. Tucked their heads under neatly folded sheets. Swam in a sea of saline and suffering. Took preposition-sized bites out of his last uneaten meal. Left marks on the crisp, white charts that could never be unwritten.

Some of them just stood out in the hallway—silhouetted against a backdrop of two inter-stitched lives now unraveling into one, with one foot in the door and one foot already gone—refusing to come into the room altogether.

"*Kid, Kid, Kidster. I was praying that you'd come.*"

For the first time ever, he looked smaller than life to me. This hard outer shell of man once fused into myth now melted into mere mortal before my disbelieving eyes. The man I thought could never break now lay before me broken. This lore of a legend left reduced to simple reality in the hard light of day. The clock on the wall, unnecessarily loud in its incessant ticking out of the seconds passing by, was an exercise in obvious.

This time we have is fleeting.

"Now, since when are you a praying man?" I teased him lightly, quietly, *sadly*, as I busied my hands about the work of refolding a blanket that didn't need fixing.

He coughed through a laugh, then winced at the pain. Laughter is not *always* the best medicine.

"Well, Kid, what can I tell you?" He wiped his mouth on a wash-cloth and instinctively checked for blood.

The very same blood that coursed through my veins. This red-cell count of heart and grit and guts and glory, the kind of pulsating perseverance that can only be made from the very center of your bones.

He looked me dead in the eye, a projector reel of memories once again springing to life to play out these scenes on the walls no longer standing between us.

"I guess some things are just worth making an exception for."

PART II

the girl
after the
trailer

a ship sailing toward
a distant shore

I ONCE TOOK A CLASS in metaphysics.

When we got to the topics of identity and continuity over time, the professor introduced the Paradox of Theseus's Ship to challenge our beliefs about just how much something can change before it is no longer the same.

Imagine an all-wood planked ship, this professor explained, that sets sail from one shore to another. As it makes its ebbing journey, a single wood plank springs a leak and has to be replaced with a spare metal plank that was thankfully on board below. Is it still the same ship? Most people would say yes.

As the ship sails onward, more and more wooden planks spring a leak. And one by one they are replaced with the spare stock of metal planks from the cargo hold. Until, as the boat gently comes to rest in the sands of the distant shores, the final remaining wooden plank is at last replaced with metal. At what point does it stop being the same ship?

Was it just past the halfway mark, when the number of metal planks officially outnumbered the wooden ones? Or was it only after the last wooden plank was replaced, when no remnants of its former self remained?

Now imagine that the sailing process from one shore to the other took ten years, such that weeks and months passed between each change and the boat had time to come to know itself as now including all these new parts. So that when it got to the other shore, looking so different and unrecognizable to those who once knew it, *it still knew itself.*

Is it the same ship then?

I don't know exactly when the Girl In the Trailer goes from being herself to being the Girl After the Trailer.

Was it the day she left home? Was it the day she made a home of her own? Or did it not happen until that day eighteen years in when she had finally spent more time out of that trailer than in it?

I'm not sure.

But I do know what it's like to be in that same boat.

I know what it's like to get to the other shore, looking so different and unrecognizable to those who once knew you, and still be able to recognize yourself. To be at once completely different and yet somehow the same. To be at peace with these new parts that now make up you, while still giving honor to all the parts that came before.

So, just how much can a person change over time without losing who they once were?

And how do we hold on to that when everything around us is letting go?

BEFORE I WENT TO YALE for law school, I spent a year in England.

And before that I spent four of the best years of my life at West Virginia University getting my undergrad degree.

But I *almost* didn't.

Growing up without a lot does something to your brain. I can't explain it. Maybe it has something to do with the prefrontal cortex still developing. Or maybe it's negative neural pathways grown closer over time at the repetition and replaying of bad thoughts turned bad generational patterns. I don't know, maybe it's just inhaling all the mildew.

Whatever it is, it makes you *expect* to fail before you've even tried.

I once heard a scientist say that if you think positive thoughts over and over, the resulting neurons will look like lush, healthy trees, whereas negative thinkers tend to end up with neurons that look like trees in the dead of winter. I don't know if that's true or not, but the visual stuck with me.

I think my trees probably look like a scene right out of *Sleepy Hollow*.

There are a lot of different ways to describe this feeling. You can call it fear of failure, being your own worst critic, being too hard on yourself, self-doubt, lack of confidence, low self-esteem, insecurity, a poverty mentality, or just a plain old pervasive sense that no matter what you do, you will *never* be enough.

Pretty fun, right?

Here's the thing. I had parents who always told me I could be anything I ever wanted to be when I was growing up. I had incredible teachers all the way from kindergarten through high school. I have studied abroad and at one of the top Ivy League institutions in the US, and still some of the *best* teachers I ever had came from the West Virginia public school system: Mrs. Barrett, Mr. Moose, Ms. Spencer, Mrs. Johnson, just to name a few. I was consistently told I was smart, consistently told I was capable. So there is no rational reason in the world why I should continue to feel this way.

But that's the thing about Fear. It doesn't operate out of a currency of rational.

So it was, my senior year of high school, with the horizon of the rest of my life laid out before me, I almost couldn't bring myself to send in my application to WVU. When I found out they enrolled twenty-two thousand students—more than ten times the number of people in our town—it is without an ounce of overstatement or hyperbole that I tell you I was absolutely *convinced* I would fail out if I went there. Convinced I would be at the very bottom of that ranking. *Number twenty-two-thousand-and-one.* The least qualified of these. I instead resigned myself to the far more manageable local community college, population 1,502.

I think I might come by this kind of thinking honestly.

Growing up, anytime I ever asked Dad about a potential solution to his troubles or trying something that would make his life just a little bit easier, he always said the same thing.

"Kid, let me tell you: *this is how it is, this is how it was, this is just how it always will be.*"

He never said it about me. Always told me my life could be different. But I think he underestimated just how much the words he spoke over himself were also absorbed by me.

Like some sort of working-man's-hands osmosis.

To a little girl who was always listening.

I've always said my dad cut the trees that built my future. And it's true.

But ultimately, we also have to ask ourselves: what kind of little trees are we *growing*?

I DID END UP sending in my application to WVU.

It was an action born out of necessity.

There is only one law school in the entire state of West Virginia, and since I knew absolutely nothing at the time about the process, I just assumed I had to attend the same undergrad university where I wanted to study law. Like one big seven-year program that was take it or leave it. And ever since I was little, dressing up in Goldie's pink Sunday school suits and watching *Perry Mason* and *Matlock* with her while pretending I had clients to meet with, I have *always* known that one way or another I would go to law school.

Now, you might think it's strange that I could on the one hand be so absolutely convinced I was going to fail out of college, while at the same time be so determined to see that law school dream come true. But therein lies the tension for people who grew up like me: a fear of failure constantly embattled with an almost compulsive need to achieve.

The girl in the trailer and the girl who so desperately wanted to exist after the trailer, both bitterly embroiled and at war with themselves. And both knowing full well that they would never forgive themselves if they didn't at least try.

Just like that, WVU was back on the table. I requested an application packet, filled everything out, and sent it back in by the first day of admissions.

It was the only school I applied to.

It never even occurred to me to look out of state.

I DIDN'T FAIL OUT OF WVU, for the record.

In fact, I ended up graduating with all straight A's all four years. Except for one B+ that still haunts me to this day.

It happened the second semester of my freshman year, in a cake-walk of a class that should have been an easy A, but I just didn't take it seriously enough. And the feeling of it—seeing those round, curved edges of a letter staring back at me from the paper where there should have been only hard lines—made me so mad that I decided to never let it happen again.

But you didn't come here to hear about grades.

More importantly, those four years at WVU were some of the most transformative of my life. I joined the debate team, took classes with phenomenal professors, made an amazing group of friends, I fell in love. All of which challenged me to see the world as a bigger place than I ever had before. A world that didn't drop off at this undulating, irregular heartbeat of a boundary that is the West Virginia state border—these rising and falling round, curved edges that had also somehow always formed a hard line in my mind. Instead, I saw a world beyond that maybe had a place for me after all.

Let me be clear here, I *love* West Virginia.

Anyone who has ever stood in a stadium surrounded by a sea of blue and gold sixty thousand strong, shouting "Let's Goooooo, Mountaineers" at the top of your lungs until you don't have a voice left anymore, knows what I mean. Anyone who has ever been away for a while and comes back to see that Wild and Wonderful sign hanging over the highway only to crank up "Country Roads" and instantly know that you are home, knows what I mean. Anyone who has ever driven up the Highland Scenic Highway in the height of fall and watched the mountains explode into so much color that it looks like they're on fire—an inferno of red and orange and yellow blazes burning down the hillside in a display that would give any New England state a run for its money—anyone who has ever witnessed that *knows* what I mean.

These mountains get into your very soul.

This leaving or not leaving West Virginia was never a question of love. It was more about seeing what was waiting for me on the distant shore. It was about who I might become in the process. Which is why in the fall of my senior year, instead of going directly on to law school, I found myself before a panel of judges in a small, windowless room, applying for a scholarship to spend a year in England getting my master's degree in moral philosophy.

Now all I had to do was break the news to JR Bess.

Dad had been one of the biggest proponents of me going to WVU, challenging me to think bigger than that local community college. But now that my eyes had turned to a world outside the state, his was also the loudest voice in the room telling me to stay. It was safe within these imposing mountain boundaries he had always known. If something bad happened, he could get to me, reach me, keep me protected. To him, the world outside West Virginia was a scary place.

And my leaving, my running, my staying gone, was maybe the first thing in his life that he was ever truly afraid of.

THE LIGHT FALLS just like warm amber syrup, like sweet honey in the rock, in Morgantown in the fall.

In the early morning hours of those earliest September days, you can climb a hundred steps if you're not careful, all before breakfast, all in the pursuit of ascending up the side of the main WVU campus sitting high up on the hill. When the climb turns you out—breathless and alive—at the top of Woodburn Circle, there you'll find yourself in the shadow of an ornate, sweeping, mansard-style brick building, proudly rising to turn its face to meet a canopy of bright blue sky above. Its clock tower ticking out all the time you have left in the world to make your home there among the mountains.

And every last second of it bathed in abundant, golden light.

It was there on the third floor of Woodburn Hall—while shifting uncomfortably in a tufted, sticky, leather wingback in the office of the chair of the political science department—that I found myself in the early morning hours of an early September day, when nothing would ever be the same.

I was there to go over a few different applications for scholarships to study abroad the next year, when another professor burst in to say that a plane had hit the World Trade Center. At the time, he believed it was just a small propeller plane that had gone off course. But a few minutes later, when he returned to say that a second plane had hit the other tower, we all knew the world had just changed forever.

By the time I left that office and made my way across campus to the student union, another plane had hit the Pentagon, and a fourth had crashed in a field only eighty-some miles away from us in Pennsylvania. A sea of us stood there together, mouths open, staring in horror at screens that weren't making any sense, not knowing where else to go. Not until they announced that all activity on campus was suspended due to the tragedy that had just struck our nation did it finally start to sink in that any of this was really happening.

We all made our way back to our apartments and dorms. Six of us in our building sat together in one living room, holding hands and praying while we watched the news unfold. We stayed that way together for most of the night until the early morning hours. Afraid to turn off the television. Afraid to fall asleep. *Afraid of what we would wake up to.*

One week later to the day, I got the call.

I would be getting on a plane to go to England.

You can imagine how well that phone call went.

Me calling Dad one week after the world stopped turning, to let him know I would be spending all the next year an entire ocean away. Although I wouldn't technically be leaving for months, to him it may as well have been the very next day for how much he thought that would change *anything* about the world now being a very dangerous place indeed.

"You can't be serious," was all he said.

Actually, that *wasn't* all he said. For the next ten months, in fact, counting down to the day I got on that plane, that's all I heard. I think he truly believed if he just said it enough times, he could talk me out of going.

"What's in England anyway? Don't they have master's programs at WVU?"

The scholarship I had been awarded was the Rotary Ambassadorial Scholarship, and it was for a full ride covering tuition and housing to spend one year abroad.

It was sponsored by the local chapter of Rotary International, which is a group comprised of business owners and professionals united for the goal of advancing peace and goodwill around the world. As a scholarship recipient, part of my duties for the year would be to visit over fifty local Rotary clubs all over the UK and deliver a talk as an ambassador of West Virginia. I would get to tell the world how much I loved my home state.

It was also the first time in my life that I experienced firsthand *rich people doing good*.

Growing up, Dad was always pretty clear on this: "There are rich people and there are *good* people, and the two are rarely the same."

I was never taught much about money growing up. Except maybe to fear it. Which makes sense given the kind of people with money that Dad was always up against.

I was maybe five years old the first time I crouched hidden in the living room of our single-wide trailer and watched him slumped at the kitchen table by the phone. It was the sort of phone—you may remember the kind—that was still connected by an actual cord to the actual wall. And it just wouldn't stop ringing.

Anyone who grew up poor knows that when the phone starts ringing, it isn't a good thing, because it means that there are people who want things from you. Bill collectors and people who wear ties to work, who always want more than you have to give. The demanding ones who seem to have a gift for knowing when there's more going out than coming in.

Maybe because it felt like there was *always* more going out than coming in.

It was maybe the tenth call of the evening that did him in. The final straw that broke his back, and I watched this giant, larger-than-life man bend and crumple and snap under the weight of trying to make a living for his family.

It was about two weeks later that the bank came and took our logging trucks. Not pickup trucks, mind you—the eighteen-wheel kind. The Kenworth and the Mack. And in our small logging community on the top of a mountain in rural West Virginia, that's the kind of thing that gets noticed.

I watched Dad get smaller and smaller as those trucks drove away.

And now here I was about to take money from people who wore ties to work. The kind of people who, in his eyes, had always been his sworn enemies. And here they were, sending me a world away from him.

This was a scholarship that had been funded by people who had earned more than enough to give away, and I could see with my own eyes that they were doing good with it. It was the first time my own thinking started to break away and drift apart from Dad's, like an ocean forming between us, our two worldviews no longer the same.

Maybe money doesn't have to make you good or bad. Maybe it just amplifies what's already in your heart.

And maybe there was actually a lot more good in the world than he was ever willing to admit.

Either way, on some level, it still felt like a betrayal.

My graduation from WVU was spread out over an entire weekend.

In addition to the Rotary Scholarship, that year I was also awarded the Order of Augusta. I know that sounds like something out of a Harry Potter movie or maybe an Indiana Jones movie, but it's not. Augusta was actually one of the original names in consideration when West Virginia seceded from Virginia and the Confederacy and became a state in 1863. In Latin, the word *augusta* means digni-fied, majestic, sacred, worthy of honor. But instead they just added *west,* and the rest of the country has been confused ever since as to whether we're a real state or not.

"What, do you mean like, *western* Virginia?"

Great Day May 2002
For the Family of
Mary Ellen Bess –
Graduating with the
Highest Honor given
By the University of
West Virginia
A Day For Mary's
Grandmother – Goldie
Bess – to Cherish Forever

"No, Jeffrey, *I do not*. Read a map."

Augusta would have probably added some much-needed clarity.

So to honor that almost-name, WVU created the Order of Augusta—its highest honor—to give out to its top eight graduating seniors each year. And I was now one of them. I had been so terrified of failing—of being number twenty-two-thousand-and-one, the least qualified of these—that I had run from that fear of failure and not stopped running until it had a new name.

And that meant that there was now a whole weekend of brunches and awards ceremonies leading up to the main event. Dad, Mom, Goldie, and Aunt Lynn were there for every one of them. And Goldie's favorite part of the whole weekend was when we were all taken by police escort, sirens blaring, to the Coliseum, where they were given VIP seating for the graduation. I could see her dandelion hair poking through the crowd, a huge smile spreading across those big apple cheeks. I think for Goldie it just confirmed what she had suspected all along: that she was in fact a *very* important person.

One part firecracker, one part sassafras.

Just a few weeks later, we all stood together in the Washington Dulles airport, saying our goodbyes.

DAD HARDLY SPOKE a word to me the day that I left.

He picked a fight with me early that morning over some silly thing, and from that moment on you could've only cut the tension hanging in the air between us with one of the two chainsaws he kept in the back of his pickup truck. He sat silent through lunch, his big hands balled into fists on top of the menu, nervously tracing the M-shaped scar on his finger and audibly sighing every few seconds. Just in case any of us forgot that he wasn't on board with any of this.

In the drive to the airport, we blew up into a big fight. One of the biggest we've ever had.

I told him to just drop me at the door, but they all decided to come in. Goldie held my hand while I went to the counter and got my ticket. She started crying as soon as we got to the newly restricted, post–9/11 security point and they couldn't go any further. She hugged me twice and wouldn't let go. Mom double-checked that I had my passport and a prepaid phone card and all the numbers written down to call when I got over there.

Dad just stood off to the side, not saying a word to anyone, staring at the cold, hard, polished ground beneath him.

I hugged Mom and Goldie one more time and then turned to go.

"Well, are you even going to tell me *goodbye*?" I asked from the brink, just before I was past the point of no return.

He sighed and hobbled over to me, his never properly healed ankles acting up again. He hugged me hard, his face buried in my shoulder.

And then the storm finally broke.

He wept.

Right there in the middle of a crowded airport.

He wept for everything he felt like he was losing and everything that might possibly go wrong. The clock on the wall, unnecessarily loud in its ticking, was an exercise in obvious.

He had been dreading this day for ten months, and he hadn't been able to stop time.

"You be careful over there. Your ol' dad loves you, do you know that?"

"I know." *I had always known.*

I gave him one last squeeze, and then I was gone. I boarded a plane that would cross an ocean.

I bet I must have looked smaller and smaller as he watched me float away.

A ship no longer safe in harbor, sailing off to a distant shore.

Mary's Family was so
Proud of her to go to England
And Study and got her
Masters At the University
of Hertfordshire - England -
But
It was So Hard at Dulles
Airport in Washington DC
to see Her Leave -
Our Hearts Just About
Broke - But it was A
Great opportunity For Her
What A Great Kid!
Our Mary

12

stories change stories

IT TAKES COURAGE to chase a dream. Raw, unfettered, lion-hearted, caution-to-the-wind *courage*.

It takes confidence and patience and perseverance too. And lest we forget, there *will* be tears. Whether proverbial or actual, we shed our blood, sweat, and tears in pursuit of these dreams. We give our everything. And then we give more.

Frustration. Failure. Fight for it and forward.

It takes all these things to chase a dream.

And in the case of applying to law school, it also takes . . . *money*.

Cold, hard, day-late-dollar-short, working man's, never enough, show me the . . . *money*.

When I started sending in my law school applications at the beginning of the year during my study abroad in England, you have to understand that each school I added to the list cost me a *minimum* of seventy-five additional dollars. Money I did not have. Just for the *privilege*, in my mind, of most likely being turned down. For the life of me, I can't remember if there weren't any fee-waiver programs back then like there are now, or if I just wasn't aware of them. But either way, my budget and my options seemed to be growing smaller by the minute.

So I started to do what I like to call *reality-check math*. It's kind of like "night math," if you've ever done that, where you add up how many hours of sleep you can get if you were to fall asleep right then, only that just ends up stressing you out more and keeps you awake longer. They are similar in that both are an exercise in stress and *scarcity*.

I don't think rich people have to do a lot of reality-check math, where you limit your own options because of the price you have to pay. But it's basically like playing the ponies. Only it's with your future. You start to look at the odds. You study the programs. You place your bets strategically, with the hope of a good showing. You're not going for the perfecta. You're just hoping that you place.

I had sent in only half the applications I wanted to, when my friend Josh—my boyfriend at the time—asked me about Yale. We were applying to law schools at the same time, and we both had reality-check math problems when it came to the money, so he knew all about it.

He waited a second while I ignored him, and then asked again. "*Seriously*." He tapped me on the forehead. "What about YALE?"

"Josh, you know as well as I do that it would be just about as helpful for me to light a hundred-dollar bill on fire and watch it *burn*, as it would be to send it off and think I had a *chance* of getting in there."

I was annoyed at him for even bringing it up again. Yale is the number one law school in the country. Getting in there is basically the higher education equivalent of finding a golden ticket in a chocolate bar. And as far as *Charlie* was concerned, I had already spent my last dollar.

But Josh being Josh, he saw a version of me I couldn't possibly see in myself. So he gathered up all the required materials from my other applications, made me sit down and write the additional personal essay that Yale required, and mailed it all off in a big, fat manila envelope the next day. With a check he wrote himself.

Josh was the first boyfriend I ever had who was truly kind to me, who showed me how I should be treated. And he had also just taken money out of his own pocket to take a chance on my future. Both of those things, it turned out, would change my story forever.

"So, what'd you write about? How much you love *ivy*?" He said it with a smile that told me he had already read it.

I had written about that trailer.

DURING MY YEAR IN ENGLAND, I studied at a small campus out in the country called Wall Hall at Aldenham Abbey, which had been the residence for Joe Kennedy when he was the US Ambassador to Great Britain in the late 1930s. It was a beautiful, old, ivy-covered stone mansion with these overly exaggerated Camelot-looking towers that made it seem like a Disneyfied version of itself. Like if you climbed up and poked the towers, they would actually be made of foam or something. Like they would topple right over at the slightest push. The whole building looked strange there in all its grandeur, sitting out in the middle of farmland, which in turn was out in the middle of nowhere. Actually, you had to take two buses just to get to nowhere.

This was something else entirely.

I was assigned to the Binghams Dorm, where I would essentially be sharing a flat—shared kitchen space, communal bathrooms—with several English students who were in their first few years of university. There were only three people total in my master's program, and the other two didn't live on campus. So that—plus the fact that we were at least two bus stops from nowhere—meant I had better find some people I could get along with, and *fast*. What actually happened is that the six of us ended up becoming the best of friends.

We became so close, in fact, that we started calling ourselves the Binghams Crew.

Now, besides the fact that they were all English and I'm American, and that they were all in their undergrad programs while I was getting my master's, there was one other important difference between us. I was the only one in the group who believed in God.

This made for some rather interesting late-night conversations.

Truth be told, I've never had a problem being friends with people who hold different beliefs from me. I've never been one of those people who can only have a friends group where we all check the same boxes and vote for the same people. It's just not who I am. In fact, maybe it's the debater in me, but I kind of *welcome* the chance to have my beliefs challenged. It's only made me grow stronger in my faith to know *why* I believe what I believe.

And the Binghams Crew offered that in spades.

On one particularly intense night, we all sat on the floor of my bare-bones dorm room—a desk, some posters on the wall, basically a cot for a bed—with the rough, industrial carpeting digging into our legs. The room looked and smelled like it hadn't been updated since the 1970s. And since we were the last group of students who would ever be studying at the Aldenham campus before it closed down at the end of that year, there was little chance of that changing now. We sat crisscross, with our knees nearly touching. Close enough so we could really see each other.

And they all took turns asking me questions rapid-fire.

I think something happens when we are humble enough to be questioned. When we are willing to acknowledge just how crazy it can sound from the outside to believe in God, if you aren't already someone who knows Him. This God floating somewhere in the sky, raining down pestilence or floods or rainbows, depending on His mood. This God turning some people to salt and giving other people bread. This God who could eliminate all evil and hunger and disease in the world in a second if He wanted to, and yet those things still exist.

I once took a class in college called The Philosophy of Religion that was taught by a devout atheist. For our final and *only* grade, we had to write a paper dealing with the problem of evil, which basically asks how we can reconcile the existence of evil and suffering in the world with an omnipotent, omniscient, and omnibenevolent God. In other words, how can we say that God is all-good, all-powerful, and all-knowing if He chooses to allow the people He loves so much to suffer at the hands of evil?

These are complicated questions, and there are a lot of ways to answer them. My answers focused on free will as the necessary component in the divine experiment between God and humans. I argued that for God to eliminate evil would also be to turn us all into some sort of super-obedient robot-angels. Incapable of ever doing evil, sure. But also incapable of ever deciding to do good or to freely love one another or to truly *choose* God, to voluntarily give our lives to following Him.

But that class and that paper and those complicated questions aren't really the point.

The point is that we can't browbeat people into giving their hearts to God. We can't thump our chest and scream in their faces and twist their arms until they change their minds. Even if we could, that's never how God wanted it. It was always meant to be a choice. A root change that happens in the heart.

All we can do is sit cross-legged and open-hearted across from one another—close enough where we can really see each other—and tell our stories.

I once heard an incredible photographer named Esther Havens say, "Stories change stories."

So I told the Binghams Crew about a God who drew close enough to leave fog marks on my windows. A God who was in the green of the grass and the mud on my hands, how once it became a part of you, you could never forget how it felt. How He was color and freedom and fire and dirt. The God I had always known as a best friend, who came all the way down from heaven and sacrificed everything just to be near to me, to be near *all* of us.

I didn't convert anybody that night. Or the next. Or the next. That was always their choice to make.

But I was the first person who ever told them what I believed not by trying to beat them with my arguments or by being the one shouting the loudest in the room. I did it with the words printed across my life. Words we drew close enough to one another to really see. *Because stories change stories.*

That's the question we really have to ask ourselves.

What story are we telling?

WHEN I WAS LITTLE, a mean boy in the lunch line once told me, loud enough for everyone to hear, that I was even uglier when I smiled.

So for a long time I stopped smiling.

A mean girl once told me from the perfectly curated platform she loved to stand on, loud enough for everyone to hear, that the world only wanted pretty stories.

So for a long time I stopped telling mine.

A mean world once told me in all its not-so-subtle ways, loud enough for everyone to hear, that good girls never raise their voices, wild and untamed.

So for a long time I got very quiet.

Then I stopped.

I stopped letting the world and other people tell me who I am.

Whether we realize it or not, every single one of us is walking around with the words someone else spoke over us tattooed on the sleeve where we once carried our heart.

What takes a second to spill from their lips—like tiny tractor-trailers crashing and colliding into one another in chain reaction, thudding out a steady drumbeat of destruction in their wake—

spends a lifetime wreaking havoc in our minds. We absorb those words. Wear them like a new skin we're never comfortable in. Take them as the truth. Memorize them like the lyrics to a song we can't get out of our heads.

They tell us that our story will never be enough. That *we* will never be enough.

But we never stop to ask ourselves, "What if they're wrong?"

Somewhere along the line, I think we've gotten away from wearing our mud on the outside. We've gotten it in our heads that if these lives we are building aren't pretty every step of the way, then we are somehow doing it wrong. We've started to believe that if it looks hard or messy or steeped in the struggle, then it won't be celebrated.

The world values different things now. Maybe it always has. Maybe the person with rough, calloused hands covered in scars from the pursuit of building a better life, leaving a trail of dirt wherever she goes, was always going to be someone on the outside.

Sometimes I think we are afraid of the dirt still caked under our fingernails from the last time we had to dig ourselves knee-deep out of the mud. We start to despise these days of small beginnings, believing that if our story doesn't measure up, then *we* will never measure up.

We carry that shame like a qualifier to our life's sentence. Modifying the descriptors as we go. Editing, revising, abridging the messy, until we've washed and watered it all down enough to ensure that we blend. Fit in. Disappear altogether if we have to. Just so long as no one sees the muddy fingerprints this story has left across our lives.

We get really comfortable with the hiding. We get really safe not being seen.

Which means it can feel a whole lot like whiplash when God suddenly takes that hard, heavy story you've been trying so hard to hide all along and uses it to start opening doors you never dreamed of.

Good. We need that kind of shake-up.

Because the truth is, when we lean into this dirt that grew us, this struggle turned fertile soil where our roots run deep, we stand a little taller. Open our arms a little wider. Turn our tired faces to the sky. Trade our shame-stories for a strength inside us we never knew we had. And decide once and for all to own *all* of it.

The hard, the gritty, the bittersweet.

This world may try to tell you it isn't beautiful.

But what if they're wrong?

THAT SPRING, as my year abroad was winding down, I thought I already knew where I was going to law school.

Over Christmas break, there were a few early-decision letters waiting on me. And from that group, I had chosen a *wonderful* school. The financial aid forms were filled out. The housing had been assigned. I was all set. My decision was made. *Done.*

But Dad still held out hope.

Somewhere in that year with an ocean between us, he had gotten on board with the idea of chasing dreams outside our boundaries. Every time I talked to him, in fact, he asked the *same* thing.

"So, have you heard from Yale yet? Have any letters arrived from ye olde Yale yet?" He said this last question with an overdone British accent reminiscent of *Masterpiece Theatre.*

I guess that's how he thought everyone at Yale talked.

It went on that way for months. And honestly, I was growing a little weary of the question.

Josh was studying at Cambridge University that year on a Gates Scholarship, and was also getting a master's in philosophy. I traveled hours by bus and train to visit him a few times that year, and the first time I set foot on campus, my breath actually caught in my chest. Cambridge was unlike anything I had ever seen before.

There were wide, sweeping, walled-in courtyards, bound on every side by stone archways and elaborate, adorned spires reaching toward the sky. The vast green spaces beyond were perfectly manicured, their intricate designs carved right into the grass, down to every blade. And when they hit the hard edge of a building, *undeterred*, they seemed to crawl right up the side, morphing at once into bright green ivy. Long stone walkways crisscrossed in every direction, traversed daily by at least one person in a long black robe running off to somewhere important. And everywhere you turned there were bells that never seemed to stop ringing. As if even they couldn't believe they were lucky enough to be there.

The River Cam cuts a path right along campus, its still waters dotted with regal swans swimming lazily in every direction, apparently nowhere *they* needed to be right away. And for a small fee, you could rent a narrow, flat-bottomed boat called a punt and push your way down the river with a long pole like a gondolier, gliding under stone-arched bridges. What they *don't* tell you, though, is that the muddy riverbed in Cambridge can often get sticky in places, like thick clay. So that while your boat glides ever onward, sometimes you and the long pole stay behind. Josh and I would spend hours like that, sitting on the grassy shores, the golden sun warm on our faces, watching the uninitiated take their first bath in the Cam.

That's where we were sitting late one sunny afternoon when I got a call from Dad.

JOSH AND I WALKED our way across campus as I tried to find a stronger signal.

In those days, doing a transatlantic phone call on a simple cell phone was no easy feat, and the calls would cut out often. But if you were patient with it and bought enough prepaid phone cards, you could more or less make it work. When the bars shot back up, I dialed Dad's number.

"Hey, Kid, how we doing?"

"Oh, pretty good. It's getting to be almost dinnertime here, so we were just deciding on a restaurant."

I felt like I was more than a world away from him now, at home here among the ornate arched buildings, choosing between one nice restaurant or another.

"Oh, sounds good, that's a fact."

I don't know why, but Dad used to end most of his sentences with *that's a fact*.

He went on that way for a few minutes, mostly making small talk. But looking back now, I know he was *fishing*.

Finally, the inevitable question. "So, have you heard from Yale yet?"

I don't know if it was from frustration with the phone cutting in and out or just being hungry in general, but my temper finally ran short with him.

"NO, I haven't heard from Yale yet," I snapped into the phone. "And guess what, I am *never* going to hear from Yale. I think maybe it's about time you give up on that and stop asking already, don't you?"

"Really?" he said.

"*Really*." I said.

"Huh. That's interesting . . . because they called the house."

"Wait . . . *what*?"

"Yeah, sure did, that's a fact. Called the house and talked to your Grandma Goldie. And you know how she is. She gave them the third degree, a full-on interrogation. But they said they could only talk to you. Left a number for you to call."

I sat in silence, my brain trying to catch up to the words still floating somewhere midway over the Atlantic.

"Okay. Well, what do you think this is about?"

"I don't know," he said, and I could hear him smiling through the phone. "But before she hung up, that Yale lady did tell your grandma she could at least tell her one thing. She said whatever it was, she was pretty sure you would be happy about it."

It took two hours and five dropped calls back and forth before I was finally able to connect with the dean of Yale Law Admissions.

When she said the words she had for me, I had her repeat them two more times just to be sure. Chalked it up to a bad connection. Even called her back to make sure it wasn't a mistake, that she hadn't accidentally called the wrong person and given me a future that actually belonged to somebody else. She just laughed across an ocean, her words at last coming to rest on a far distant shore.

"Mary, welcome to Yale Law School."

belonging is a gray j. crew sweater

THERE COMES A TIME in every story when the hero finally gets everything they ever wanted. And that's usually when the music swells and the credits roll or the last page turns or we just flip the channel. I believe there's a reason for that.

We don't want to spend too much time with somebody once they've gotten everything they've ever wanted. They become insufferable. They become unsympathetic. They start using words like *whom* properly in a sentence. There's no more mountain left for them to climb, so we're out.

We're underdog people. Get out of here with your *all my dreams already came true* nonsense. Just take your football and go home, *Rudy*. Go live your happy life and let us be. We're already on to the next unlikely story.

But what if success was where the real trouble began?

What if we got everything we ever wanted, only to find out it doesn't change a thing about not liking this skin we have to do life in, this dirt still caked under our fingernails. That once we go home and tuck ourselves between the cool cotton sheets, where it's just us and the darkness settled in, it hasn't changed a thing about how easily we can lay our heads down and fall asleep at night. We feel like a fraud, a walking, waking imposter. And we hate ourselves for still feeling this way. If anything, it just makes us hate every raw, exposed nerve ending all the more.

"You should be better than this," we whisper to our thin epidermis. "What on earth could you possibly still be screaming for? You have *everything* you ever wanted."

The hero, it turns out, is flawed. Deeply, deeply, deeply flawed.

And no amount of success is going to undo that. No relentless pursuit of more is going to erase what was missing. It's going to take digging in and doing the hard work of healing if there's any hope of changing all that. But how do you gather up the nerve when it already feels so damaged? And is that the kind of story anybody will ever care about?

Plot idea: our hero tries to overcome the insurmountable, in this awe-inspiring, stand-up-and-cheer, true-life, feel-good story of the year, by becoming . . . just *ever so slightly* less flawed. Still flawed, for sure, but just a *little* less broken by the end. Maybe there's a dog. Maybe she takes up yoga. Or cooking. Possibly needlepoint. Or she just gets really, really good at naps. There's definitely a lot of coffee on account of all the naps. And wine, *plenty* of wine. I wonder if Diane Keaton would be on board to play the lead.

Yeah, I don't know if that movie would ever get made. I can't really seem to hear the rising crescendo of a score as the credits roll.

We don't really make movies about what happened *after* someone got everything they ever wanted.

About what happens when the hero at last has to come face-to-face with what no amount of success will ever fix.

But that's the story we're living now.

THE FIRST TIME I set foot on the Yale Law campus was with Dad and Goldie. We had all piled into his red 4x4 Ford truck and made the ten-hour drive from Fenwick Mountain to New Haven, so that I could try to find an apartment before classes began in less than a month.

Dad had called me on one of my last days in England and told me to pull up the Dodge website. He had me click on the Neon model, he told me to make it red, had me add a spoiler to the back and upgrade to the CD-player option. And about ten more things I don't remember after that.

I was growing impatient.

"That's great, Dad. It's really cool that the website will let you do all that. But I gotta get back to packing now."

"Ten-four, I won't keep you . . . I just thought you might like to see your new car, Mary."

He jumped on the stunned silence.

I'm not sure if it was more from the car or the fact that he had just, for the first time in my life, called me by my given name.

"So now do you want the good news or the bad news?"

"Well, *both*, I guess."

The car I drove in college had been sitting in the gravel driveway next to the trailer for the past year while I was away, where I assume it continued to chip paint and turn rusty, just like it had for the previous four years. It was this purply blue color, so synonymous with the late 1990s, that was known for widespread chipping and thus widespread recall. We had it repainted once, courtesy of the manufacturer, but it was chipped again within a few months. So we just let it go. A purply blue rust mosaic in the form of a compact four-door. Also, when I was driving home from Morgantown a year earlier, a big bunch of "Congrats Grad" graduation flowers had tipped over and dumped in the back seat. And the last twelve months spent sitting in the sun had done absolutely nothing to dissipate that dirty, flower-water smell.

"The good news is, you're going to have a brand-new car to take up there with you to Yale, so that none of those rich kids can turn their nose up at you. It won't be anything fancy like they probably have, but at least it will be new, *that's a fact.*"

Looking back on it now, I think he just didn't want that familiar smell of mildew following me to Yale Law School.

"Oh, wow, that's amazing! Thank you *so* much! So what's the *bad* news?"

"The bad news is, I picked it up over there at the dealership and had gotten no more than five miles out of Summersville when I hit a deer and dang near totaled the whole thing."

"The car or the deer?"

"Well, *both* I guess. I mean, the deer didn't make it. He's dead, deader than anything. The car is going to survive. But it's going to be over there getting put back together until the day before you leave for law school."

So that's how we found ourselves, less than one month before classes began at the top Ivy League law school in the nation, driving around New Haven in Dad's filthy, mud-caked, 4x4 pickup truck with a chainsaw, empty gas cans, empty Dr Pepper cans, and a bunch of dozer equipment filling the bed to the brim.

We parked that red truck on a side street right next to the Yale Law entryway, with all its stone archways and its gargoyles looking down on us and laughing from their lofty positions on High. And I couldn't help but stand in the shadow of the contrast.

I felt as out of place there as that red truck looked.

The first time I set foot on the Yale Law campus, I didn't even dare walk through the doorways to go inside. I was afraid they would take one look at me, at that truck parked out on the street, and realize what a terrible mistake they had made in letting me in. Instead, I just walked to the side of the building and pressed my face against the window, peering into a future that still looked like it didn't belong to me, preserved and untouchable there behind the stained glass.

For now, looking in from the outside was going to have to be close enough for me.

Eventually, we all return to dirt.

When I went back home to Fenwick Mountain for those few weeks before classes began, what I was struck by most was how everything seemed unchanged. This former life of mine stood there perfectly preserved in frozen time. In my old bedroom in the trailer, there were the same stuffed animals stacked on a shelf just like they had always been. There was a bottle of perfume still knocked sideways and shattered on a little side table—the careless breaking from someone trying so hard to leave in a hurry—as if it had been there waiting for me to come back home and pick up the pieces. There was a pile of sweaters still stacked on the floor, folded and gathering dust, from when I couldn't fit them in my suitcase a year before. It was like they had been there the whole time with hopeful, foolish eyes fixed on the door, looking for the slightest sign of my return.

Everything was still exactly the same except for this subtle descent into disrepair.

Have you ever noticed how rotting is sometimes the only witness we have to the passing of time?

Think of an abandoned house left to itself for a hundred years. What do you see? The ceiling and walls caving in. Wild vines growing through the floor, crumbling the carpet in their wake. The breakdown and disintegration of everything it once was.

Standing in that trailer, I couldn't help but wonder how long it would take until the weeds and wilds of the mountain reclaimed it. Swallowed it whole back into the deep, dark woods that surrounded it. Until the snakes and the mice and the ground itself did what they wanted with it.

Eventually, *everything* returns to dirt.

A few weeks later, I returned to New Haven with a put-back-together, cherry-red Neon to start classes at Yale Law School.

The previous May, while I was still in England, a bomb had been set off at the law school during spring semester final exams. So now there was extra security posted at every entry. I can tell you, this did absolutely nothing for lessening my fear that I would surely be turned away at the door.

But I wasn't turned away.

Instead, I was given a welcome packet, a student ID, the Yale Law Bulletin with its catalog of rules and courses, and a canvas bag emblazoned with the law school's bizarre crest that always looked to me like Eddie, the dog from *Frasier*, playing croquet with a crocodile.

And then I joined the rest of my new classmates at the end of the main vaulted hallway with its carved wood walls for orientation in Levinson Auditorium. The auditorium's gothic-style stained glass windows contain the various state seals, and from where I was sitting I could clearly see Connecticut, New York, and Massachusetts— even Georgia, South Carolina, and California. But try as I might, I couldn't see West Virginia in that room.

This also did absolutely nothing to reassure me.

The room we were in had a seating capacity of 450, but since Yale Law is known for its incredibly small class size, I sat there as one of only 198 men and women admitted to the Class of 2006. From the podium at the front, the dean welcomed us and told us that every single person sitting in that room had been selected on purpose and for a reason. That although it was perfectly normal to be sitting there feeling like we didn't belong, we should rest in the knowledge that each one of us added something very important to the makeup of our class. I glanced nervously around the room, looking into the faces of my new classmates.

I was pretty convinced I was the *only* one sitting in those seats that day who felt that way.

THAT NIGHT I HAD DINNER with my "small group."

The admissions staff divided up our entire class into smaller groups of twenty people or so, who would have every single class together that first semester. The idea being that it would make law school feel a little less lonely. After that first day of orientation, we gathered at the home of our contracts professor, who was also in charge of shepherding our small group, and made awkward cocktail party chitchat over passed hors d'oeuvres in the front foyer of his beautiful, grand Victorian home.

At the end of the evening, we sat crisscross in a circle, the polished hardwood floor digging into our legs. Nowhere near close enough to really see each other.

We were asked to go around and say one interesting thing about ourselves. I felt my heart start pounding in my chest—from what I could tell, it was hitting an RPM just one step below exploding—and my palms went insta-sweaty. They were sweating so much, the Yale cocktail napkin I was holding on to for dear life started to stain my fingers royal blue. That's one way to blend in, I guess. *Breathe. Just breathe.*

As we went around the circle, my very accomplished classmates mentioned things like working on the Hill for various senators or interning at big New York City law firms. My heart was thudding out a familiar rhythm in my ears now. Country roads, take me home, because this is clearly *not* a place where I belong.

When it came around to me—in a recurring stress dream somehow turned real-life—I blurted out something about bleeding blue and gold, being the daughter of a lumberjack and the granddaughter of a coal miner, and how I liked to eat tomatoes from the garden whole like apples.

The entire circle stared at me.

Their blinks made actual clicking sounds against their eyes.

Three painful seconds of silence turned eternity ticked by.

West Virginia had just arrived at Yale Law.

ALL OUR CLASSES that first year had, in varying degrees of intensity, what is commonly referred to as the "Socratic Method," which basically just meant the professors would call on you at random and keep calling on you until you refined your answer or got it wrong in front of the entire class, whichever came first.

It is *exactly* as stressful as it sounds.

There's a reason why Socrates was poisoned.

In the first week of our Civil Procedure class, for example, we started off by studying this case called *Tickle v. Barton*, which just so happened to take place in West Virginia. So the professor decided to assign it to me to present the facts of the case for the entire class. It wasn't so bad, and I lived to fight another day. But it just so happened that the case also turned out to be one of those "black letter law" cases that kept coming up again and again all semester long. I can't tell you how many times that professor would snap his fingers and point to me.

"And why is that still true, Mary?" he'd ask.

"*Tickle v. Barton!*" I'd shout. All the while praying that he hadn't actually just asked me how my weekend was or something.

There's this thing that happens to us when we're afraid.

At least, it happens to *me*.

It's like my brain is too busy screaming in decibels not suitable for human ears about how afraid it is—about how not-enough and disqualified it is before it even begins—to actually slow down and hear the question.

It reminds me of this time in fourth grade during a spelling test, when I missed hearing what the teacher said for one of the words. I got so panicked over missing that one word, that I missed the next one, and then those two dominoed into the one after that, all the way down the line.

It's sort of like that.

Our fear just dominoes into more fear.

I can't tell you how many times driving down to class that first year, I had a pit in my stomach that I was pretty sure was turning into an actual ulcer. I just wanted to turn around and go back home. Pull the blankets over my head. Get the notes from someone in my small group.

We do that, don't we?

We get so afraid of failing, that we would rather not show up to our own lives at all than risk showing up and getting it wrong. Than risk putting ourselves out there not knowing all the answers. We automatically assume every other person around us is so much more qualified than we are.

But what if we just slowed down long enough to really hear the question?

What if we silenced the screaming voice of doubt in our own head?

What if we *felt* the fear but showed up anyway?

BELONGING IS A GRAY, cashmere blend J. Crew cardigan. Paid for at full price.

Just down the tree-lined side street branching off from the law school, where an elm canopy curtsies and bows to the stone-arched architecture and wrought-iron bars of one of the world's most beautiful gated-communities-*cum*-college-campuses, there was a small shopping district at the corner of York and Broadway. There you'd find a used bookstore, a new bookstore, and an overpriced, franchised faux-French café where, if you weren't careful, you could spend your entire student loan on hot coffee and stale croissants just because of how it made you feel. Like some combination of Elle Woods meets *You've Got Mail* in every "Autumn in New England" movie montage ever made. Like the plucky underdog who just might find her way and prove everyone wrong, all before the credits roll.

Next to that was a pizza place that had been there since the sixties, with pictures on the wall like Jim Morrison's mugshot when he was infamously arrested onstage in New Haven and George H. W. Bush smiling sweetly in his Yale baseball captain's uniform. A picture of rebellion next to a picture of legacy.

And I somehow couldn't see myself in either.

Around the corner from the pizza place and the faux-French café was the official Yale gift shop, and right next door to that was the *unofficial* one, which was where all the really good stuff was. Sweatshirts and T-shirts and hats, all emblazoned with the iconic Y, and an array of colorful scarves that made it look like we were bound directly for the Sorting Hat. It was all there, everything you needed head to toe, to tell the world which school you now belonged to. And more importantly, to tell the world who it was you were becoming.

But for me, the real Yale Law uniform was found two doors down in the form of one gray J. Crew sweater.

It sat, perfectly folded in three-part harmony, on a pin-lit shelf above a rack of freshly sharpened pencil skirts. Every button was fastened, gold medallions glinting in the halogen light, and inside the fold was the crinkle of tissue paper that whispered to me how no one else had ever owned it before.

It belonged only to me.

It was only two weeks into classes when I swiped my card and bought that gray sweater, without another thought of how long that money actually needed to stretch. It was the most I had ever paid for a single article of clothing, and I took special pride in the fact that I had paid full price. This seemed to me like a rich person move. Rich people don't wait for sales. When the word *Approved* flashed across the screen, the lady at the register tucked my receipt in a tiny square envelope, wrapped that sweater in even more tissue paper, and sealed it with their logo sticker—the J. Crew stamp of approval.

Without ever knowing anything more about them, this *felt* like what people who go to Yale would do.

It was certainly what people who go to Yale wore. Two weeks of classes had taught me that much. Everywhere I looked was a gray cardigan—sometimes over a bright blue button-down, sometimes over a white scoopneck T-shirt, but the gray was always the same. And now I was one of them.

Nearly two decades later, I still have that sweater. Even though that kind of gray has never looked good on me. Even though the threads have started to unravel in places, revealing holes when you hold it up to the light where once there were tightly stitched seams. Even though it now sits in a drawer and takes up space—this clutter we tend to hold on to, these versions of us we once thought we had to become in order to belong.

When I think back on this now, I can't help but remember this short story called "The Necklace" that I once read in Ms. Spencer's seventh grade English class. The basic plot goes something like this: a woman trying so desperately to belong borrows a fancy necklace from her wealthy friend only to later lose it at a party. Based on appearances that can be so deceiving, she assumes that her friend's necklace must be real diamonds. So she buys a replacement necklace on credit and spends the next ten years in poverty paying it off. When she runs into her friend all those years later, just after the last payment has been made, in relief she confesses what happened and everything she's had to sacrifice in order to pay off that necklace. Through tears, her friend takes her by the hand and explains that all along the original had been a fake.

Mere costume jewelry for a woman playing the part.

I don't know why that story sticks with me so much, but it does. Of all the plays and short stories I have surely forgotten through the years, that one stays vivid in my mind. Perhaps it's because I don't know if I'm more like the woman who lost something along the way in this pursuit of trying to belong, or the one who has become so comfortable faking her way through life in the first place. Maybe they are just flip sides of the same coin, and that's the point.

But either way, this constant filling up of things—this stockpiling of *more* to try and silence a deep hole of unbelonging—is a debt we can spend our whole life trying to pay.

And I can tell you this: none of it is the stuff that lasts.

Because the first day I wore that gray sweater to school, when I walked through the stone-arched doorway, past the mahogany desks and tufted leather chairs, I could still swear I smelled the slightest whisper of dollar store vanilla perfume.

It turns out, the only thing that does fill—the only thing that does last—is a debt that has already been paid for. At full price.

And it's offered to us for free.

I WISH I COULD SAY that gray cardigan was the first and only time I tried to fill a deep, ugly hole in my heart by buying pretty things.

It wasn't.

But when I think of that sweater in particular—its stiff, sewn-in tag scratching at the back of my neck, clawing at my backbone with all its crisp newness—what I remember most is how it didn't make me feel different, like I thought it would. The cashmere-wool blend itching on my arms only served to remind me that I hadn't also, somewhere in the process, been able to zip myself out of my own skin and step into somebody new.

I was still me. Just me in a gray sweater.

Also, I'm not sure "hole in my heart" quite captures it either.

For me, it's always felt much bigger, more like a hole through my entire torso. Like that movie *Death Becomes Her*, where you can look straight through Goldie Hawn and see that where guts and backbone should have been, it was now just gaping, hollow, and empty. Like a sucking chest wound left naked and exposed, raw nerve endings recoiling at the rush of cool air. It reminds me of when I had two wisdom teeth pulled, and the pink, quivering sockets of bare roots it left screaming in their wake. Trying so hard to solidify and close over, but tearing loose again and again at the slightest word. These ripped-out wounds that refuse to heal.

It feels like a root canal the size of a chest wound.

That's what it was like for me to walk around in the world with a hole in my heart.

I suppose when I look back at it now, that's really what I was trying to do. Trying to stuff my life so full of things and achievements, of capes and costumes and masks, that they would pile up and accumulate and somehow backfill that hole. Like a landfill of gold stars and brand-name labels, the temporary hits of my preferred drug of choice that seemed to numb but never satisfy. Where *numb* somehow still seemed like enough.

I guess that's because back then, I wasn't so much concerned with healing as I was with just silencing the exposed roots.

A lot of the time, to be honest, I could forget that hole was even there, could forget I was walking around and people could see right through me. But when the air hit it just right and the temperature changed in the room, it would knock the breath out of me every time. Send me screaming back into myself. Every nerve ending—itching, scratching, clawing at itself—on full display.

People do all sorts of innocent-looking things to try and fill the holes they carry. They perform and achieve, drink, shop, spend, scroll, watch TV, and pretend like they're living someone else's life. Some people get really good at being good, like if you're good enough nothing bad can ever happen to you again.

I think at the time, I just wanted God to keep the wins coming, like some sort of never-ending Pez dispenser doling out success. A daily hit of the good stuff, this concentrated sugary-sweet high of getting everything you ever wanted. This manna of *more*. I didn't want God bothering me with little things like what might actually nourish me or just how anemic my faith had become.

Just keep the candy coming, God.

So I shouldn't be surprised that in the years to come, it was not so much a filling but an *extraction* that I would end up needing most.

a constellation of complicated

I met Justin the summer after my first year of law school, when I had already decided I was never getting married.

My parents had been separated for fifteen years or so, that summer I turned twenty-four. But they were only now getting around to talking seriously about making it official with an actual divorce. This was both a relief and a hurricane.

For a decade and a half, they had kept up a very tidy parting of ways. It was amicable. It was more or less mutual. And they could pick right up where they left off anytime they saw each other for a holiday or one of the weekends when Mom was back home.

Like Mom said to me once, her face relaxing, softening at the edges in a way that tells me it was the truth, "Your dad was my first love. I will probably die loving him. We just can't live together."

They had the most unusual marriage I'd ever known. But now that they were staring down the barrel of the actual end, it seemed to me that they were having a pretty typical divorce. Feelings were hurt. Tempers ran high. There was the occasional spat over the division of assets, of which there were not many. I had taken Property Law that 1L first year, and for the record, it proved to be of absolutely no help whatsoever when it came to dividing up a life together.

For the most part, they left me out of it. It was a hurricane, but more like one of those hurricanes you watch on TV, where Jim Cantore or some other guy in a blue parka can barely be heard shouting into his microphone over the roar of the storm, while you watch safely from the comfort of a couch in your living room. A fishbowl for your observation, where you know there's devastation, you can *see* it, but it feels like it's somehow confined behind the glass where it can't touch you.

A ship in a bottle. Wreckage in a hurricane vase. A tempest in a teacup.

Still, their marriage and now their impending divorce had been enough to convince me that I didn't want any part of either of those things for myself.

Maybe I hadn't escaped unscathed after all.

I told them as much when I was back home for Christmas after my first semester of law school. Goldie got us all a block of hotel rooms four hours north, in Wheeling, West Virginia, so we could drive through the twinkle lights at Oglebay Park. Dad's favorite.

I was fresh off a breakup with Josh, and as Mom, Dad, and I sat together with our feet in the indoor hot tub at the nice hotel with its crystal chandeliers and red-velvet-clad Christmas trees—three fish out of water, since none of us had thought to bring bathing suits—they speculated over whether we would get back together. Mom had been certain Josh and I would eventually get married.

"Honestly, guys, I don't think I *ever* want to get married."

My words were drowned in a sea of "Oh, one day you'll change your mind," the irony apparently lost on them.

"No, really, if this is how marriage ends, no offense to you guys, I just don't think I want any part of it." I liked this new matter-of-fact place we had arrived at with one another. Three grown-ups navigating a new normal with our feet in very hot water.

And that's exactly where I still found myself that following summer. Happy to meet new people, happy to make new friends, but no real interest in marriage.

Which made it an especially inconvenient time for me to meet my future husband.

JUSTIN AND I AGREED to meet at a coffee shop in downtown New Haven called Koffee Too, which no longer exists. It has gone through multiple iterations since then—all of them coffee shops—and is now currently called Blue State Coffee, for obvious reasons. Connecticut is one of the bluest states in the union.

West Virginia, now one of the reddest.

Technically, we had met online two days earlier, when I was only one day into a three-day free trial of Match.com. One day in and meet your future husband—it was like I had won some sort of online dating lottery. He winked first, which, if you don't know, is a thing you do on Match to say hi. *How you doin'?*

He was *virtually* flirting with me. I winked back.

I remember my profile name was *marypoppins* and then a bunch of numbers, because every other combination of marypoppins had already been taken. Apparently I scored no points for originality. I hoped to at least do better with the "about me" section.

A good friend of mine wisely informed me, "No matter what you write, it's going to sound cheesy." He was right. Every intro I write sounds like a "hopeless romantic seeking nice guy type with 100k salary and 2k ring" entry in the classifieds. So I guess I'll just go with the truth. I just want to have fun and meet new people. Two things that have been seriously lacking since my move to CT. I'm an official homegrown West Virginia girl. I love my family because I can talk to them like friends and my friends because I can fight with them like they're my family. I tend to be a bit of a free spirit. I can't imagine living my whole life in just one place. I admire people who grab life with both hands and aren't afraid to just hop on a plane to wherever. I love people who make me laugh. I love to make people think. I absolutely hate writing a "dating intro" paragraph.

I wonder if it's possible to retroactively die of embarrassment. I'm asking for a friend.

Driving down to meet up with him that day, I expected to feel panicked. I was, after all, meeting up with a stranger from the internet, and that was back in the days before that was something people really *did* just yet. Was he the future love of my life or a serial killer? At that point, it could have gone either way.

But I didn't feel panicked. I felt peace washing over me in waves. I felt it when I put on one more coating of lip gloss before heading out the door. I felt it when I got in the cherry-red Neon to drive downtown. I felt it when I rounded the corner and saw a brown-eyed boy sitting at a high-top table by the window. He had a camera laid out in front of him—our version of a red rose—so that I would know it was him.

"Justin?"

"Hi, Mary." His whole face was a smile.

I had never seen somebody smile like that. Where it wasn't just his mouth, but his eyes, his cheeks, his forehead. Even the dimple in his chin. It was as if his entire face was happy.

And as somebody who'd always had just a little bit of sadness behind her eyes, this intrigued me greatly.

WE SAT IN THE COFFEE SHOP and made small talk for a while. And then we got our drinks to go so we could walk around New Haven and I could show him my favorite buildings on campus. While he showed me how the light fell across them in a way I had never noticed before.

We had winked at each other on a Tuesday.

The coffee was on a Thursday.

We went hiking that Sunday.

By Monday, we were married.

Just kidding.

It would be a year and a half to the day after that first coffee—which, as it turns out, Justin doesn't actually drink—that he would get down on one knee, under an old apple tree I used to climb as a child on Fenwick Mountain, to ask me about forever.

But hold on a minute. We're not there yet.

JUSTIN COMES FROM a long line of happy marriages.

His grandparents Cuneo were married fifty-three years. His grandparents Marantz for forty-eight.

And then there are his parents, who met the night after high school graduation and now, forty years of marriage later, are still just as happy and in love as those two crazy kids who found each other one fateful night at the boardwalk down the Jersey Shore.

Growing up in a home like that changes you, does something to you, down to a structural shift in your DNA. It's like you've been bitten by a radioactive spider. Only instead of being able to leap and swing from tall buildings, you're left with a supernatural security in who you are. A spidey-sense for a quiet, assured confidence and a rock-solid foundation on which to stand. Justin doesn't have an ounce of ego, neediness, trust issues, or jealousy anywhere in his body.

In other words, *the exact opposite of me.*

I think maybe that's why Justin caught me so much by surprise that summer I was sure I never wanted to get married.

The truth is, being with Justin was never really a decision. At least no more than the earth decides to rotate around the sun or we decide to let gravity have a pull on us or two magnets decide to snap together with a force that makes it impossible to pull them apart.

Every part of me is happy just to be in his orbit. His is the kind of gravity that pulls you in and makes you feel rooted, but still lets you know what it is to fly. And the forces that snapped us together to begin with only get stronger over time. I'm pulled to him. Anchored to him, like a ship that's safe in the storm. And sometimes when we sit on the couch together and I press the side of my face against his, I get what the magnet was going through.

It's like you always want to know what it is to be just a little bit closer.

He's the rock in our team, but he never forgets that rock would be nothing without the roll. And I'm that high-wire tightrope walker who always remembers how lucky she is to have him as her soft place to land. I'm up and I'm down and everywhere in between, and he just stays the course, steadily pushing us, moving us further along the journey.

I asked him once if he ever wished he had met a girl just a little less broken. One with fewer scars. Fewer dark places in the twists and turns of the deepest hallways of her heart. Less emotional baggage that, once left unpacked, opens up again and again like an old wound grown familiar, faithful only in its stubborn and steadfast refusal to heal.

I asked him if it wouldn't have just been easier if *I* had somehow made it easier. Had come to the table with an easier story to tell. A suburb. A happy home.

To which he replied, "I love your scars like I love your dots."

Dots are what he calls what I want to say are freckles but are in reality just moles. Freckles would be much cuter.

"When I connect them, it maps out who you are."

And in that moment, I thank God again for the man He sent. One who sees flaws and cracks in the facade as the places where the light gets in.

A constellation of complicated that is ever thankful to have him as her True North.

I SEE LOVE because I have known love.

Quietly and fearlessly and without question.

In the moments when it was most uncertain. In the times when it was most undeserved.

I have been loved when I was wrong, and I have been loved when I was angry. I have been loved when, like a wild-eyed animal— scared and clawing at anyone who tried to get close to me, leaving marks all across the wide-open palms of the hands that tried to hold me—I ran back to the comfort of the deep, dark holes I like to hide in. I have been loved at arm's length, when I wouldn't let anyone get any closer. And I have been loved through closed doors and brick walls and the battered, barbed-wire barricades around a heart that had grown so weak and world-weary, just sick to death of breaking.

I have been loved when I was tired—like parched, dry bones that didn't have the strength to stand. And I have been loved when I found myself on the floor. Those times when I buried my face in an old sweatshirt and cried angry, salty, stinging, bitter tears. They ran down my face without apology, and with each crashing aerial drop I felt the weight on my shoulders growing heavier.

I have been loved when I didn't trust. I have been loved when I couldn't breathe. I have been loved when every cell in my body was screaming out about how it couldn't go on.

My life with Justin can be summed up with these words I play like a record loop in my burning brain. I have tattooed them on my heart.

I have been loved. I have been loved. I have been loved.

In the deepest part of my heart, this is how I believe God loves us too.

I think for the longest time, so much of my pain—my striving, my performing, my running—came from this deep belief that I had to be more of something before God or anyone else would choose me. That I had to hide those parts of me that were insecure, angry, petty, or envious in order to stand before Him. Like He somehow didn't know all those things about me already. On some deep level,

I believed I needed to be the kind of person who was never in any particular need of prayer so that I was never a bother to Him. I thought I needed to achieve and achieve so that I could stand before God and He would see I hadn't been a waste of His time. A waste of His sacrifice.

I thought that when He looked at my scars, He saw flaws. But the truth is, He just saw my story. And every little thing that was broken was a chance for Him to make that story beautiful. Every wound was an opening for His light to get in.

He sees it all, and He just reaches out again with His wide-open palms that have held me.

I have been loved. I have been loved. I have been loved.

And that, it turns out, changes *everything*.

WE STOOD SURROUNDED IN LIGHT, a million stars hanging in the quilted sky.

That last year of law school, Justin went home with me to West Virginia for the few days leading up to Christmas Eve. And that night, just before we packed the car to drive to New Jersey to be with his family on Christmas Day, he asked me to go for a walk in the snow.

When we stepped through the back screen door of Goldie's little red house, the whole yard was covered in a crisscrossed pattern of luminaries. Candles glowing warm, casting a million glittering, in-candescent reflections on snow-covered pickup trucks, junk piles, and worn-out old tires. It was the most beautiful I had ever seen our yard.

The candles led down toward the trailer in a long wide arc, then back up past the toolshed and the woodshed and the place where the swing set used to be. Eventually they ended in an orb of golden lights encircling an apple tree. The same old apple tree I used to climb as a little girl.

A meandering, littered, lighted path that now indelibly stitched my future and my past.

The first time I ever knew I was going to marry Justin was three weeks into dating, when I came down with the worst stomach flu you can imagine. It was like the first five minutes of *World War Z*. Brad Pitt crashing into things, trying to get somewhere fast (I'm guessing the bathroom), being chased down everywhere you turn by the walking dead, a little girl in the back seat screaming, "I want my blanket!"

It was a plague of apocalyptic proportions.

When Justin came to the door bearing gifts of saltines, ginger ale, and applesauce, I refused to let him in to see me that way. Three weeks of dating is not yet stomach-flu serious. So he sat outside in the hallway for the longest time and talked to me through the door. When I finally let him in—ghostly white, shivering with a fever, hair plastered to my forehead with what I want to say was sweat but was most likely vomit—he didn't even think twice about crossing the room and wrapping me in the first blanket he found.

It was the quilt on my bed, alternating squares of pinwheels and pink hearts. It had been started by my great-great-grandmother on Mom's side, then worked on by my great-grandmother, and Goldie had it finished for me just in time to send me off to college with it my freshman year. Three generations of women on both sides of my family had stitched their mark in that blanket Justin wrapped me in.

And now here we stood under a quilted, starry sky. A patchwork of light and darkness bleeding into one. My future and my past finally at peace with all the pieces that had made me.

I stood there in the snow, both the Girl In the Trailer and the Girl Who Came After.

And they both said yes to forever.

BACK INSIDE, Goldie was the first one we told.

She was busy stirring chopped apples into her homemade stuffing when we walked in, preparing to cook the turkey overnight for Christmas dinner the next day. And it made me feel guilty all over again that we were leaving. Mostly it made me miss the turkey, stuffing, and white bread sandwiches that she and I always snuck and ate on Christmas morning before anyone else was up.

Goldie was nothing if not a traditionalist, but with me she was always willing to bend the rules.

Christmas Eve she would get up every hour on the hour to check on what she affectionately called "Tom Turkey." And in my later teenage years, I had taken to staying overnight next door at her house so I could get up with her each time. Sometimes we would just stay up together all night. Goldie peeling apples in long curlicues and us watching *I Love Lucy* in black and white.

We would leave Nick at Nite on all night, the blue glow of the TV casting strange shadows on the tree, the vintage orange-and-red bubble lights raging back in full color. I could stare at those lights for hours. Glass eyedroppers filled with food coloring water on top of cheap plastic bulbs, percolating with nostalgia. They had to be at least fifty years old.

It would always take them a while to warm up, but once they did, everything in the room changed.

"Grandma Goldie, we're getting married!" I held the ring up in front of her face, a move I had seen a thousand different times in a thousand different movies.

I had an *idea* in my head of how this was supposed to go.

She looked down the bridge of her nose through the bifocals in her glasses so she could get a better look. When she did this, her chin would almost entirely disappear into her neck. Then she looked back up at me over the rim of her glasses, sizing up the situation, a stern, serious look flooding her round face.

She started nodding her head, a bobbing motion gaining momentum like she was winding herself up to something.

"Okay, we can do this. We can *do* this."

Everything in Goldie's Appalachia was something to get through. To survive unscathed. To live through long enough to fight another day. There was no doubt in my mind she was already adding up the cost and making a list of everything that needed to be done. A checklist of how to get there.

So in Goldie-speak, "we can do this" was the same as if she'd just said, "Congratulations! I'm so happy for you."

I interpreted this for Justin, who had not yet learned to speak the secret language that my grandmother and I shared.

From there we went around the room, hugging an aunt, an uncle, a little cousin who was so excited to be a flower girl. But one room over, by the Christmas tree in the living room, Dad sat stoic in the rocker recliner, bubbling with emotion and not talking to anyone.

Justin had talked to him earlier in the day, asked him if it would be okay if he asked me to marry him. Dad nodded his head quietly and shook Justin's hand.

"Well, I reckon that would be alright."

But now that the moment was upon him, his only daughter about to leave him for good, he stared at the ground and said nothing rather than risk breaking down.

"Dad, what do you think about all this? Pretty exciting, huh?"

Nothing.

"We're going to have to get you measured for a tux. I wonder if they make one in flannel."

Silence.

"Hey, maybe we can even dance to Dolly Parton for our father-daughter dance."

He just stared at the floor.

Since he wasn't talking, there was nothing left to do but pack up the car and say one last goodbye to everyone.

I was almost out the door, almost totally gone, when the flood-gates finally opened, a torrent of tears once again breaking loose in Goldie's kitchen.

Dad grabbed me and hugged me hard, hot tears leaving streaks in the dirt that was still on his face. His chainsaw-grease hands wrapped around both of my shoulders and dug in, leaving smudged fingerprints across this moment in my mind. He held on and didn't let go. And his whole body shook with the quiet sobs he had been holding back all day. Sobs, if we're being honest, he had probably been holding back since the day I was born.

His wet cheek pressed up against mine, and he whispered hard in my ear, "I am *so* proud of you, do you know that?"

We stood like that, father and daughter, holding on to one another for a long time. And then I got in the car and drove away with my future husband.

The warm glow of Christmas lights behind us. Everything still bubbling to the surface. A constellation of complicated wrapped in a blanket of quilted stars.

I always had an *idea* in my head of how this was supposed to go. But looking back now, I wouldn't change any of it for the world. It had been the perfect reaction for my family.

They weren't big on fancy. They didn't always know the right thing to say. It would always take them a while to warm up to a new idea.

But once they did, everything in the room changed.

substance over surface

ONE OF MY FAVORITE CLASSES in law school was Federal Income Taxation with a professor who *quite literally* wrote the book on it.

You might think that sounds about as interesting as watching dirt gather dust, and at first glance I would have been inclined to agree with you. We were, after all, going to be spending our days reading line by line directly out of the United States Tax Code. *Section 1401. Subpoint (b)(2)(A). Little roman numeral i.*

It was going to be *riveting*.

Except that it actually was.

This professor had a way of zeroing in on a normal, unassuming-looking piece of code that most people would have skipped right over and seeing something else. The story behind how it got there.

Where most people saw a tax break for a certain kind of vehicle, she saw a powerful lobby at play influencing Congress. Which brought up questions about fairness and transparency. Where most people saw tax benefits for being married filing jointly or a deduction for claiming dependents, she saw a bigger conversation about what a society values being codified directly into the law.

She was tough.

She would call on you and keep calling on you until you didn't know the answer to something. But I think she only did that to teach us some humility that we didn't always know all the answers. That things weren't always as clear-cut as they seemed on the surface.

One of the biggest things she taught us to look for was substance over form.

And I *adored* her for it.

I suppose that's because I always wanted someone to do that for me. To look closer at the story beyond the surface and see something else there, something other people had always skipped right over. I wanted them to see the substance I held before an opinion was formed. To lean in and understand everything that had to happen in order for me to get there. I wanted someone to recognize the inherent value I stood for.

Rather than just how easy I was, on paper, to classify and write off.

WHEN I WAS STILL IN COLLEGE, Goldie had to go in for open-heart surgery.

The doctors gave her only a ten percent chance of surviving the operation—she needed both a triple bypass and a valve replacement—but they told her there was a *hundred* percent chance she would die without it. And so, against those kinds of odds, she opted to have the surgery.

The surgery itself actually went fine, and they were able to repair her heart. But something happened on the way to calling it a success. Every time they tried to close up her chest, her lungs would collapse and her heart would stop beating. Time after time they tried, and time after time they would lose her. Until the only thing left they could do was to leave her that way. And *wait*.

For twenty-one days they kept Goldie under anesthesia with her heart, and her chest, wide open. Day after day, they poured entire jugs of antibiotics directly into that open wound. And for twenty-one days, the experts on the situation—the doctors and surgeons and hospital administration—started talking to my family about the options and the odds. And they got really good at using words like *can't*.

She can't possibly last much longer.

She can't possibly come back from something like this.

She can't possibly go on.

But they didn't know the kind of heart that they were dealing with.

Because on the twenty-*second* day, they were able to go in and close her up, and she went on to make a full recovery. That surgery bought her another ten years with us.

Goldie taught me a lot of things throughout the years, but that story in particular taught me this:

You have to be willing to be the CAN in your own life.

Because there will always be an abundance of people more than willing to tell you that you can't. You have to be willing to go up against those kinds of odds, even when no one else can see it. You have to be willing to wait out those open wounds and let them heal in their own time. You have to be willing to speak truth to every voice of doubt around you, whether it's from the experts or the voices in your own head.

When those doctors met Goldie, they didn't know the kind of heart that they were dealing with.

But that's the kind of heart that beats in me.

It's the kind of substance you'll find pulsing there right below the surface.

ONE OF THE MOST prestigious things you can do while studying law in New Haven is to go out for the *Yale Law Journal*, which is the school's best-known law review and is generally thought of as a necessary stepping stone to clerking for the Supreme Court.

I did *not* go out for the law review.

Instead, I auditioned for the Yale Law *Revue* (see what we did there with the spelling?) which was the big end-of-year sketch comedy show that was a mix of songs, skits, and prerecorded videos, in a very *Saturday Night Live* sort of way. For the writers, we started working on the show months in advance, getting together over fried food and cheap beer to draft out sketches, seeing what stuck, throwing out half of it, and starting all over again. And we would spend the last few weeks of the year, when we were supposed to be studying for finals, holed up in the auditorium and rehearsing that show till all hours of the night. One year, we even drove all the way to Cambridge, Massachusetts, dressed as six-foot-tall lobsters, and tried to get admitted to Harvard Law.

In other words, I had found my *people*.

I auditioned my 1L year by putting together an impression of one of my other favorite Yale Law professors, who I *loved* and who also had a tendency of *pronouncing* her punctuation.

"When the Court overturned this decision *comma* what they were really saying *comma, emphasis added* for the first time was that a law that discriminates on the basis of sex was unconstitutional under the Fourteenth Amendment. *Period*."

We had a lot of fun with that.

"When the Court overturned this decision *comma, hyphen, exclamation point*, what they were really saying *apostrophe, semicolon, open bracket*, for the very first time, *emphases, parentheses, ellipsis . . . dot, dot, dot . . .*"

It was probably a lot funnier in person.

Either way, that audition not only helped me make Law Revue that year, but one of the skits I helped write actually became one of the openers for the whole show. It was of that same professor doing a *properly punctuated*, equal rights reinterpretation of "Baby Got Back."

By 2L year I was one of the directors, and by 3L year I was awarded the most coveted spot as one of the two news anchors on our own version of SNL's *Weekend Update*. That year, it went to me and my blonde friend Ashley—Yale Law's answer to Tina Fey and Amy Poehler, who happen to be the first and only all-female duo in *Weekend Update* history.

We liked to think my punctuating professor would be proud.

ONE OF THE BIGGEST THINGS I learned from doing that show is this:

Funny people also tend to be hard-story people.

It's as if the people who have experienced some of the saddest things in their stories want to do everything they can to make other people laugh.

I have this theory that we're all born into the world with these hard edges, these sharp corners we're all walking around with. And when we bump into other people, without ever meaning to, we leave cuts on them. These cuts can look like a harsh word or thoughtless comment, an act of selfishness, or forgetting to include someone. It can be as simple as walking through this world and not recognizing the magic of every other human spinning wildly through space alongside you. Every day we're out there doing this. Bumping into each other, leaving our marks.

Death by a thousand cuts.

But, *my very scientific theory goes*, something also happens to hard-story people that softens them. Like progressively finer grit from sandpaper, pain rounds off the hard edges. Where selfishness and thoughtlessness once lived, empathy moves in and takes up residence. It puts some flowers in the windowsill. It unlocks the front door. Kindness and gentleness are then born out of a genesis of scar tissue and become the foam bumper guards that allow us to lean in close and see others in the midst of their pain.

We can now get close without cutting. We have become a soft place to land.

There is a reason why some of the most funny, beautiful souls you'll ever meet are people who have known brokenness. I used to wonder what it would be like to be a totally easy-story person. Someone who grew up easy. Went to school easy. Started a business and it was always just . . . easy.

There was a time in my life when, if someone had given me a magic lamp or the ability to snap my fingers and swap places with someone else *Freaky Friday*–style, I would have taken their easy story in a heartbeat. I wouldn't have been able to snap my fingers fast enough. But somewhere along the way, that all changed.

I think it was the moment I realized that if I could somehow change my story overnight, but in doing so would have to give up being every bit of the kinder, gentler, more empathetic person that it made me—well, that was a trade I was no longer willing to make. And looking back now, if God had granted me that magic genie wish to swap places overnight, I would have missed out on *so* much He still had in store for me.

I was seeing only a chapter and wishing for a different book. Every sentence felt like a prison term. Every adjective described the wrong kind of scene. I felt like a background character in my own life. The last page, an already foregone conclusion.

But we learn to trust the story when we learn to trust the Author. And He's not done writing yet.

DAD DIDN'T COME to my Yale Law graduation.

He wasn't hurt or in the hospital. He wasn't sick, and he wasn't stuck in traffic. He wasn't out of the country or working deep undercover somewhere, and he hadn't taken a vow not to travel to Connecticut. You know, like a vow of silence. Except instead of swearing off speaking, you would be swearing off, *I don't know*, argyle or something.

It wasn't any of those things.

He just . . . *didn't come.*

In the weeks leading up, every time I asked him about it he just said the same thing.

"Oh y'know, Mary, that would be like taking an old work mule to the Kentucky Derby. I wouldn't know what to do around those Yale people. All's I'd do is embarrass you."

If you would have asked me two weeks before, and one week before, and even one *day* before, I would've sworn to you that he was going to change his mind. There was no way he would miss the final step in my education, something he had worked his entire life to see. Of course he was going to be there.

Except, *he wasn't.*

When the day and the hour came, he wasn't there to see it. When Sandra Day O'Connor spoke to our class about building bridges, he wasn't there to hear it. When I walked across that stage in the middle of the Yale Law School courtyard, wearing a black robe and the purple tassel that meant I now held a Doctor of Jurisprudence degree, try as I might, I couldn't see a West Virginia logger in that crowd. Goldie was there. Mom was there. Aunt Lynn and her family were there. Justin and his parents were there.

But JR Bess missed it.

He said it was because of the dirt under his fingernails. His muddy blue jeans and an old gray suit that had long since faded. He said it was because of the truck he drove and the boots he wore. The accent when he spoke and a logger's lack of social graces. I told him I didn't care about any of that; it just meant he knew what a hard day's work looked like.

All he could see was surface, where I saw only *substance.*

Sometimes it's other people who write us off, and sometimes we write *ourselves* off before we even give other people a chance. The truth is, Dad didn't know what to do around Yale people. He saw them as a different breed of person that he couldn't relate to. A class of people he wasn't comfortable being around. The kind of people he felt embarrassed to be with and wanted no part of.

The only problem was, wasn't *I* now officially one of those Yale people too?

I was at a place in my life where I was now becoming more Girl After the Trailer than Girl in the Trailer. My life was in Connecticut now. My life was with Justin. There was a wedding to plan and a new future we were starting. I was slipping further and further away from that girl Dad knew. And he seemed to think he was doing me a favor by opening his hand and letting me go.

So, true to his word and true to form, he didn't come. And now I was left wondering if he would even be there at the wedding.

It was the Kentucky Derby of graduations, and he missed it.

Stubborn as a work mule.

THAT SUMMER, as Justin and I stood looking out on the horizon of the rest of our lives, two paths diverged before us.

On the one hand were two offers at law firms in London and New York with six-figure salaries, plus bonuses, plus benefits.

On the other hand . . . *wedding photography.*

We had the chance to start our own photography business with not a penny to our name nor a clue what we were doing. Just a dream in our hearts of an extraordinary life that was always worth the risk. But *extraordinary*, when you really think about it, breaks down to just *extra*-ordinary, *more* ordinary. And we wanted something totally different from that. So we chose *unordinary*, the polar opposite of ordinary. We chose to be the CAN in our own lives.

A year after that, we were married.

And a year after that, on our first anniversary, I wrote down some words about what that leap has meant to my life. That it's not just how we look on paper but how *we got there* that matters.

He drinks orange juice with his chocolate cake.

Orange juice. As in, the juice from an orange. From the bottle. *Simply Orange.* Country Stand. Pulp free. Orange juice. And chocolate.

It baffles me. Confuses me. What would the "Got Milk?" people say, for goodness sake.

And yet, it's just one of a million small, little, barely noticed, what's it matter, who's to say, out of the ordinary, unordinary nothings that make our marriage what it is.

He pushes me with his orange juice and chocolate cake. Challenges me. To see the world differently. For all that it could be and *never* what it's supposed to be.

And I owe my life to that.

This life that we've built. This world that we've created, where he and I alone reside. A world of soft pillows and soft places to land. Of blankets pulled up all the way over our heads and "no one will ever find us in here." A world of doing what you love and being what you love because it's what you *could* be and never what you're supposed to be.

Of being challenged. Of seeing the world differently than it looks on the surface.

I owe my life to that.

On our wedding day, we stood together in front of our friends and family and promised forever. And when it came time to celebrate, you can bet the cake was chocolate.

And everything that has come to stand for.

16

the heavy chains
we never asked to bear

I OFTEN FIND MYSELF praying two prayers, run-on sentence style, un-ironically and in the same breath.

God, I have too much.

God, when are You going to give me more?

On the one hand, I'll find myself suffocating. Sputtering and gasping, unable to breathe with everything weighing on my lungs. Like a two-ton to-do list sat down on my chest and refuses to move until I give it treats of endless checkmarks and infinite highlight reels.

Sometimes I feel like I'm drowning, breathless at the busyness of an overscheduled, overcrowded, overmanaged life of my own making.

It's all too much. But it's all too little.

And that's exactly when I ask for more.

God, when are You going to give me what *they* have? When will my life look just like theirs?

You're messing it up, God, and I know better than You do. Please give me less, God.

But please, oh please, God, *when* will You give me more?

GOLDIE COULD DO THIS THING where she could peel an entire Golden Delicious apple in one long, continuous curlicue without once ever breaking the spiral.

It was mesmerizing.

She'd sit in her recliner rocking chair, a bowl in her lap, knife in one hand, fruit in the other, and we'd share an apple together. A slice for her, a slice for me. And we'd talk about life.

She'd tell me again about the time a dog bit her when she was just a young girl. Took hold of her hand and wouldn't let go, nearly bit all the way through by the time they got it off her. And then, just like always, she'd show me the scar on the palm of her hand, and I'd trace the shiny, blanched-white skin with my own tiny fingers, feeling how the raised lines seemed to write their own history. The way these unexpected brutalities always do when they sink their teeth deep in the middle of a young life and won't let go.

Goldie never liked dogs after that.

She kept one chained up outside. A black-and-tan bear of a dog named Sebastian that was some mix of Australian Shepherd and mutt and that she inherited when someone brought him home and couldn't keep him anymore. Even as a puppy this dog was a maniac, biting at your heels till he drew blood every time you walked by, so that as he grew, the only thing containing him—and I use that word lightly—was a rusty garden chain tied to a stake in the ground near the woodpile.

He broke loose often.

He'd go running all through the neighborhood, tearing down the pavement of Airport Road, his rusty chain dragging behind him so fast, you could swear you saw sparks. It would take hours to catch him again. Mostly you just had to let him tire himself out enough until he could be tackled and returned back home to his shackles. Twice he was hit by a car; he seemed to just shake it off and keep on running.

Goldie never bought a single bag of dog food for him, but he ate his fill of scraps and seemed to be especially fond of her brown beans and cornbread. The woodpile was covered by a small wooden roof that jutted out from the back of the house, so at least he could stay mostly dry. And occasionally, when it snowed and got really cold, she would let him sleep just inside the back door chained to a hook on the wall.

She kept him because she said he was a good guard dog, but that was his entire life. He wasn't a dog that was played with or patted on the head or ever told he was a good boy. He never got toys or had someone brush the mats out of his fur.

And the longer he stayed like that, tethered by those chains, the meaner he became. So that no one could get too close to him without getting hurt.

He was a giant of a dog who lived a hard life, and it turned out he died as hard as he lived.

When he finally did get sick with whatever it was that killed him, it took three solid days for him to die. In the meantime, he convulsed and whimpered and whined. He panted and foamed at the mouth, and to be sure, he felt every ounce of pain. He left this world in the only posture he had ever known: fighting. He should have been taken to a vet. Should have been wrapped in a warm blanket and given medicine till he didn't feel anything, then had a family who loved him hug him and kiss him and tell him he was a very good boy while they held him tight and let him go.

That's how it should have been.

Instead, he died just as he had lived. Mostly alone, tied to a stake in the ground, tethered by the heavy chains he never asked to bear.

THE LAST TIME I SAW GOLDIE, it was Thanksgiving. The last breath she took came ten months later.

We were four years into our photography business at that point, and business was *good*. We were traveling all over the country, and even the world, photographing people on their happiest days and teaching other new photographers how to do the same. We were speaking in the really *big* rooms at conferences and had even put together our own cross-country tour—NYC to LA with twelve stops in between—just us, a sound system, and a trailer hooked to the back of our brand-new SUV.

We were at that stage in our business where people knew who we were when we walked into rooms—as long as those rooms happened to be filled with people from our very small slice of an industry. They had read our blog, knew our work, asked if they could take a photo with us. A couple times people even shook and cried when they met us, telling us what our posts and teaching had meant to them. It was surreal. And it was like cool Vicks VapoRub to every crackling, sizzling, on-fire synapse in my desperately-seeking-to-be-important-and-have-my-life-matter-for-something brain. Simultaneously soothing and exhilarating, it made me feel like I could breathe again. A thick salve of self-importance to some very old, gaping wounds.

We were deep in this business of being important when Goldie started to decline. A few ministrokes here and an infection or two there, and they decided to move her over to the spare bedroom at Aunt Lynn's so she could be watched round the clock. This was where she was waiting for us when Justin and I made the trip home to West Virginia that Thanksgiving.

We spent two days with Goldie, eating turkey and playing board games. We even picked up a pizza—pepperoni and banana peppers, our favorite—for what we called "Second Thanksgiving." She couldn't really get out of bed at that point, so we just stayed by her bedside. When it came time for us to leave, she sat up on the edge, skin on bones in an oversized sweatshirt, and we took a picture together.

"Take a photo with me, Goldenrod." She always *hated* when I called her Goldenrod.

She had lost so much weight, and they had cut her hair so short, that her ears stuck out extra wide on either side of her head. At the same time, the medicine she was on had caused her big apple cheeks to swell even more. She was both Goldie and not Goldie. A mere caricature of the woman who helped raise me. We smiled in black and white—me in a scarf and hat, already busy about the business of leaving—and something inside me already knew this was the last picture we would ever take together.

And I was right.

Even though ten more months passed before she was gone.

Grief does strange things to a heart. It convinces you of things you know are not true. Maybe not on the surface, but deep in your soul and your lower intestines, where guilt twists and churns and bubbles up, your truest conscience demanding to be heard. But grief whispers louder. It hisses and purrs in your ear, lulling you into versions of yourself you never believed you could be.

It tells you things like, "This is how you want to remember her. You don't want to be there at the very end. It will be too hard to see her like that. It will ruin every good memory you have of her if you end on such a horrible one."

And so I stayed gone. And I got really busy being busy so I wouldn't have to think about how my heart was breaking. I talked to her often on the phone, of course. Even when they moved her to the hospital, even when there were so many tubes in her mouth and throat that I could barely understand a word she said.

Even when she asked me to come.

I stayed gone. *Gone, gone, gone.*

And then she was gone too.

Grief and distance did absolutely nothing to spare me from heartbreak. Every good and beautiful memory was still coated in the pain of knowing that never again would I feel her warm, soft, scarred hands. Never again would I watch her peel a Golden Delicious apple in one long, continuous curlicue without once ever breaking the spiral. Never again would I watch her laugh so hard it didn't make a sound anymore, till tears streamed down her face and her whole body shook at how funny it was.

Now there was just silence.

And the heavy, black smoke of regret curling around each memory, dimming its golden light.

Never again made worse by *wasn't there.*

TEN MONTHS AFTER we took our last photo together, Goldie took her last breath. I got the call while I was photographing a wedding, in the morning while the bridesmaids were all downstairs laughing. It was Mom on the other end of the line.

"Mary, it's your Grandma Goldie . . . *honey*, she's gone."

I closed the door to a spare bedroom and cried violently for my grandmother for exactly five minutes. Then I wiped my face and smiled through the rest of a twelve-hour day. Three days later, I delivered her eulogy at the small, red-velvet-clad funeral home to a room only half full of people. A few of which might have preferred it if I'd just stayed gone.

I mourned my Grandma Goldie for a solid year before I stopped finding myself facedown on the floor. It was years after that before I could look at her letters again. And through it all, this is what I learned.

Grief is a liar and an ocean. Just when you think you've reached the shore, it rises up again and swallows you whole. Weeks can go by without any tears at all, and then an unexpected card stuck in a book can knock you flat on your face sure as any tsunami. And your throat burns and sputters and chokes, drowning in a torrent of salt-stung water, as you gasp for air and try so desperately to wake up from this dream. But then the tide goes out, and your sobs fade to quiet whimpers, like foam sinking into sand, as reality washes over you again. Till there's nothing else you can do but pick yourself up and start swimming for shore once more, knowing full well the next wave is not far behind you. Calling to you like a siren in a swell. Beckoning you to go under. Inviting you to drown in the depths of their absence. Grief is both an ocean and a liar.

But it is also, in its own broken way, *beautiful*.

Losing Goldie taught me that we don't get to skip out on the pain if we want to keep the good. That the good is only as good as the hardest times we've walked each other home through. And if we want someone to know what love came down looks like, they'll know us by our scars.

YEARS AFTER WE LOST GOLDIE, Justin and I found ourselves in a cold, fluorescent emergency vet's office, unexpectedly saying goodbye to Cooper, our dog of twelve years. We got him as a puppy, and for about as long as there had been a Justin and Mary, there had been a Justin, Mary, and Cooper. We didn't make sense without him.

As I buried my face in his thick golden fur, tears soaking the shaved spot on his paw where the needle would go, I couldn't help but think of Goldie and everything she had taught me.

Goldie left this world in the same posture she had spent most of her life: fighting fiercely for her family, even when it meant carrying heavy things she was never meant to bear. She was the first one who ever told me about Jesus, but she spent a lifetime *teaching* me about Him, only using words when necessary.

And through both her life and her death, she taught me this: We don't skip the pain because that would be easier. We lean into it because that's what love does.

And it's some of the most *important* work we'll do.

Cooper left this world wrapped in a warm blanket and was given medicine till he didn't feel anything. He then had a family who loved him hug him and kiss him and tell him he was a very good boy while they held him tight and let him go. And this alone felt like an act of revolution in my family. A tree of generational change.

We got to bear witness to this entire life, start to finish. We were there holding him the day we brought him home, and we were holding him the day we let him go. He was loved fiercely from day one to day last.

And I can tell you this.

The bitter end did nothing to undo all the beautiful that came before.

I will spend the *rest* of my life wishing I had done that for Goldie.

17

not even real dirt

ATTICUS IS THE NAME of my favorite bookstore-café in New Haven.

It sits at the corner of the High Street entrance to Old Campus, just across the street from the Skull and Bones not-so-secret society, and has hands-down the best black bean soup you'll ever find anywhere. One day, as we waited for our table to be wiped down, I flipped through a book from the staff picks shelf up near the front of the store called *T-Rex Trying*.

It was about all of these seemingly ordinary things that become much harder when you think about T-Rex trying to do them with his tiny arms. T-Rex trying to catch the bouquet at a wedding. T-Rex trying to jump rope. My favorite was how sad T-Rex was trying to play the bass guitar, and how happy he was when he found a ukulele.

I thought about T-Rex again years later, the first time I found myself on unfamiliar ground, talking to God in a new way.

My friend Karen, who was also a photographer at the time, had announced a new conference she was starting in the fall of 2012 for

Christian creative women. And she was looking for speakers. I was a speaker now, so I reached out to her.

As my fingers hovered over the keyboard, basically inviting myself to join her conference lineup, I knew that I should have been feeling embarrassment at my audacity. Instead, it was more like an out-of-body experience—fingers typing words my brain hadn't caught up to yet, like I was doing something I was always meant to do.

I'd had a few experiences like that in my life by that point—times when I couldn't quite explain why I was doing something, but a peace washed over me in waves, telling me I was right where I was supposed to be. I felt it the summer I was supposed to be studying for the LSATs so I could apply to law school that fall of senior year. But my hands had other ideas. They snapped that workbook shut so fast and so suddenly that it scared even me. Instead I ended up taking a year off to study in England, and it became one of the best years of my life.

I felt it that warm day in June when I drove down to a coffee shop to meet a brown-eyed boy I'd just exchanged winks with on Match .com who later ended up becoming my husband. I felt it when we turned down six-figure law firm offers in London and New York so we could start a new business together from the ground up. And I felt it when we walked into an abandoned 1880s Colonial with massive water damage and a serious mold problem, and knew in my gut that we'd just come home.

It's called peace that surpasses any kind of *understanding* for a reason.

When I sent that email off to Karen, the *whoosh* sound telling me it was too late to take it back, I didn't have to wait long for a response.

"Mary! I am *so* glad you wrote! It's so crazy, because I had been feeling like I was supposed to reach out to you too, but I just wasn't sure where you were when it came to God."

She wasn't sure where I was when it came to God.

It made sense.

Up until then I had mostly kept my faith to myself. Not because I was hiding it but more because it seemed to me like a truth self-evident. Faith to me had always been more like breathing. It was something I did, not something I talked about. And yet, I had always thought that if you looked at me close enough, you could somehow tell that I had a heart for God, just like you could tell that I was breathing. It was a part of me—as essential as the steady rise and fall of my chest—but the movements were subtle, unassuming, human. You had to lean in if you wanted to see it, get close enough to hear it for yourself. *Breathe in, breathe out.*

It was a whisper, not a shout.

I reached out to Karen for that conference because I thought it was something I could do to help. I was offering a skill I had—being a pretty good speaker—for a really good cause. But make no mistake, I was going there to help. Not to *be* helped.

Give your plans to God and just watch how He laughs.

From the first moment I set foot on the Winshape campus in Georgia, I knew I had gotten it backwards. God brought me to that hillside to have my life changed forever.

Our first night began with what the program listed as "worship." In all the churches I had ever been in, I had never experienced anything called worship, so I just assumed it meant "sermon." That night we were going to kick off with a one-hour *sermon*. Maybe sing a hymn. But mostly just sit with our hands folded neatly in our laps.

So you can imagine my surprise when a band came on stage and the first guitar riffs filled the auditorium. And you can imagine my even greater surprise when everyone around me started standing up and raising their hands. They were crying and swaying, both hands raised high over their heads like they could touch the rafters. They were unhindered, unrestrained, un-self-conscious, as they reached childlike open hands toward heaven.

I, on the other hand, stood near the back in the darkness, elbows tucked tightly against my sides like one of those unsure girls in a deodorant commercial, and reached two hands up barely higher than my shoulders. Eyes darting side to side like a wild, scared animal, embarrassed at the effort.

T-Rex trying to worship.

WORSHIP WAS NOT the only thing that conference introduced me to.

Somehow, in all my years of going to church, I had never once that I can remember been taught about things like quiet time or how to study Scripture, or even that as Christians we are called to Joy.

For some reason, we mostly spent a lot of time talking about ancient people with weird names like Nebuchadnezzar. I was led to believe that guy would come up a lot more in my day-to-day walk with God. So far it hasn't been an issue.

To be honest, Joy had always felt like a party that I wasn't invited to. A mask that fake people slapped on and hid behind. A costume that matched the character we were all supposed to be playing. Joy was a strategic, open-mouthed half-laugh in every online photo. A box to check so you could stand in the right circles. A "they won't know us by our scars, they'll know us by our smiles" wax religion. Something that only shiny, happy people do.

Joy felt like a secret society, and I wasn't a member. It also felt like something I wasn't built for. Down to my bones.

Like my arms weren't big enough to pull those particular strings.

And that while it was seemingly so easy and ordinary for everyone else, it became much harder in my own restrained hands.

AFTER THE WORSHIP WAS OVER, another one of the speakers, who had been sitting a few rows behind me (and decidedly to the right), came up and sat beside me.

"You know, I've been praying for you for a while now." She put an earnest hand on my shoulder.

I blinked my confusion at her. I wasn't aware I had been in particular need of prayer.

To me, her words sounded like an indictment.

"It's just that you and Justin have such a great business, and you are doing such great things." She leaned in close for this next part, like she was letting me in on the secret. Inviting me into the society.

"I just think if you started including God more in your business and your messaging, you would be *unstoppable*." Her eyes widened at this last part, wild at the possibilities.

And there it was.

It turns out that being a Christian who actually talked about it came with its own version of performance, gold stars, and a checklist for more success. Evidently it was possible to get an A++ in evangelism.

And apparently I had been operating at a solid C−.

I left the auditorium that night with my cheeks burning hot in the cool Georgia autumn air—half indignant, half humiliated—the way you do when you find out your friends have been discussing you when you weren't around. This woman was *discussing* me to God.

And her conclusion was that I needed to be more of something—maybe more of *everything*—if I wanted to speak on His behalf.

More mentions, more volume, more taglines, more fluent Christianese.

In other words, and what it felt like at the time, more of the *same*.

If I wanted to fit in with Christians who talked about being Christian, I was going to have to be just like them.

And this was especially hard for a girl who had always felt different, a girl who always felt like on some level she didn't belong.

A girl who had secretly wondered all along if somehow she hadn't been enough of something for God.

I REMEMBER THE FIRST TIME I decided to try to put on more Joy.

As if Joy was a perfume sample I tried on briefly at the mall and liked so much—how it made me feel to walk into a room smelling like distilled righteousness—that I decided to buy a travel size so I could carry it with me at all times. An easy application for a quick cover-up. A potent enough aroma of pep in my step to cover all manner of bad days.

I could even picture the poster advertising this perfume. It hung above a metal rack stacked full of bow-tied gift sets. For a limited time only, buy this Joy perfume and get a companion pack of Prosperity and Peace for free, plus this random canvas tote bag. Which I would inevitably take home and hang on the handle of my closet door along with the other twenty random canvas tote bags I already own.

In the poster, some actress whose movies I've never seen sits in a puffy dress, in the middle of a half-laugh, in the middle of a field of pink wildflowers. Except there's nothing wild about them at all. Every single one is a forced bloom from a temperature-controlled greenhouse. Beautiful roses in every shade and variety—as long as they are all pale pink—planted in fake floral foam.

Not even real dirt.

For a while there, it felt like everywhere I turned I was running into this message that in order to be a good Christian, we needed to walk into every room and overpower people with the smell of our Joy. It would be even better, these messages screamed at me, if they could smell it before they even saw us coming. Like Abercrombie in the mall. If we could have forced-hot-air vents pumping out the fragrance of our faith, amplifying it to every passerby, then we would surely draw more people in.

The first time I decided to try putting on Joy like that, Justin and I were driving to a faith conference where I was to give the opening keynote the following morning. Thus far that day, we had already faced all manner of bad traffic, bad weather, and, well, bad

manners—and we were only halfway there. We decided to pull into a Cracker Barrel for a reset and some much-needed cornbread muffins. And while Justin went inside to put our name in, I decided to lie in the cool grass and try to get my Joy going again. I would plaster that happy face on if I had to. That's what people who wanted to give opening keynotes at faith conferences just had to do, right?

And then it happened.

I had no sooner sat down in that grass, no sooner lifted my eyes to the now blue skies above me, than something just jumped up and bit me *Forrest Gump* style. It was a bee. Bumble, to be precise. And it got me right in the, shall we say, *upper* back thigh area.

That's right. The first time I tried to put on Joy like it's something that you wear, it ended up biting me in the backside.

Because that's what happens when we try to use Joy to mask, to cover up, but never to actually heal.

Now that I think about it, I probably tried to put on a different kind of perfume back at Yale. Maybe the air of being worldly. Or the fragrance of being sophisticated enough to actually belong. Or the scent of being deep and intellectual in that chew on the end of your glasses and casually drop Jean-Jacques Rousseau into everyday conversation sort of way. *What, like it's hard?*

It turns out, I have tried to wear a lot of different perfumes in my life. Ones that make me look happy, ones that make me look smart, ones that make me feel like I belong. And let's not forget the actual ones that smell like dollar store vanilla to try and cover up the very real smell of mildew.

Either way, it's not fooling anyone.

And either way, that's not how true Joy works.

True Joy doesn't overpower. It doesn't accost someone until we are the only thing they can smell in the room. True Joy is a breath of fresh air. It is a permission to breathe easier. It is an invitation, not a full-scale assault on the senses.

It also isn't an overdesigned, overstaged, mass-marketed picture of perfection. To me, true Joy is like a tree planted by the water.

It *gives* more oxygen than it takes. It provides shade and shelter to those who want to come and sit by it for a while. It is a welcome place of belonging. A much-needed respite for the weary. A place to come and rest their tired souls.

One of my favorite Scriptures is Jeremiah 17:8. My friend Erin sent it to me when we were wading, neck deep in the mud, through one of our hardest, most heartbreaking times of loss. When I thought I'd never breathe again. When my lungs burned at the very idea of going on. When no amount of perfume faith would have ever healed.

The verse says, "[They are] like a tree planted by water, that sends out its roots by the stream, and does not fear when heat comes, for its leaves remain green, and is not anxious in the year of drought, for it does not cease to bear fruit."

Joy was *never* only for those found laughing in a field of flowers. It is also for anyone who finds themselves weeping in the thickest part of the weeds.

Joy doesn't mean the drought won't come and the storms won't rage.

It just means that when they do, you'll know where you're planted. You'll know what it is you're anchored to.

And trust me, when that happens, you'll be glad it was never fake floral foam that held you.

18

it's safe now for you to rest

DESPITE MY INTERACTION with that other speaker, I loved that first conference my friend Karen put together.

I kept going back, sometimes several times a year. And for the first time in my life, something much deeper in my faith really started to take hold. I was meeting people who were teaching me how to dig in to Scripture and to really pray about things, how to have an actual daily relationship with God, and how true Joy doesn't have to look like a plastered-on plastic smile reserved only for the shiny people. That God is not afraid of our questions or our tears; He just welcomes the conversation.

It was also on my third time at this conference that I first met Kim.

Kim is a professional goals coach who lives right outside Atlanta. She specializes in showing people that our goals are not so much about what we are achieving as they are about who we are becoming in the process. She is also a powerhouse packed with a punch when it comes to faith.

I was introduced to Kim by my friend Hannah, who had worked with her while writing her most recent book. Hannah knew that

I also wanted to write a book, and so a quick email introduction was made. A few weeks later, Kim drove up from Atlanta to meet with me in person while I was at Winshape for the conference. We sat together in an empty side room in the lobby, next to an old-fashioned popcorn cart.

And as I nervously built walls out of white, fluffy kernels spilled on the table between us, I confessed every stronghold that was keeping me stuck.

I told her about this movie I'd just watched where someone was talking about pecan trees. About how, left to its own devices, a pecan tree will keep producing fruit until its branches grow so heavy with the good things it's holding on to, it will split right down the middle. It will break its own back in its constant pursuit of more.

"*I* am a pecan tree," I told her, blinking through salty tears. "I am breaking my own back just trying to show that I am capable of good things. And it's keeping me too busy—spread far too thin—to do the things I truly feel called to right now."

Kim thought on this for a moment. Took one bite of popcorn and then another.

"I think your problem is that you're just scared to give away the fruit."

My eyes went wide at the sting of the punch. No one had ever landed a blow on me quite like that before—so quickly, so sweetly. I felt like the wind had been knocked right out of me. And I kind of liked it.

"Well . . . how do you mean?"

"I think you are believing the lie that for people like you, people who have had a hard story, there's just a set number of good things that will ever happen to you in life. A set number of good things that God has for you, and when they're gone, they're gone. And to give any of them up now, even the ones you don't really need that much anymore, is to risk that nothing good will ever happen to you again to come and take their place."

She said these last words as if they were being punctuated with a clap after each one.

Nothing. good. will. ever. happen. to. you. again.

I stared at the table, nodding, tears falling on white fluffs.

"You've been holding on so hard to these things with clenched fists. But the truth is, in trying to hold on to them, all you're really doing is letting them rot on the branches, right?"

A picture of an apple tree and Goldie's face flashed in my head. Fast, like a slide advancing, and then it was gone.

People of necessity learn not to waste any unexpected bounty God sees fit to put in their way, Mary Ellen.

Hers had always been a version of God that seemed *quick* to withhold good things.

And I guess it turned out that I was even more like Goldie than I thought. Always holding on, preparing for the worst. Expecting bad news to come knocking at the door any second.

Kim went on.

"My grandpa grows pecan trees. Do you know what happens every year when they cut those branches back? *His neighbors eat pecans.* Here's the thing: you're worried about stockpiling. You're worried about avoiding the pain of pruning. But just think of all the people who could be fed when you give your gifts away."

She let these last words sink in, let them hang for a little while longer in the salty, stale air between us. Was I trusting the good things in my life or the One who grew them in the first place?

"Your problem is, you're putting your faith in the fruit."

I HIRED KIM on the spot that day.

And the first thing we set about doing in that first year together was dismantling this ticking time bomb of a belief I had held in my hands my entire life, that told me I was only as good as my latest achievement. That when I walked into any room, it was my latest accomplishment that walked in first to introduce me, like a personal butler announcing each guest. In my head, my butler wears a top hat, a waistcoat, a tuxedo jacket with long tails, an ascot, and suspenders.

My butler is also Dwight Schrute from *The Office*.

And he goes before me into any room and announces why I am a person worth talking to. Not because of my inherent worth as a human. Not because I have a good story to tell. Not even because of my witty sense of humor, old soul, or kind heart. It's because I've done something, achieved something, that would make me a good person for them to know. I can bring them value, connections, exposure. Therefore, *and for this reason only*, I'm worth paying attention to.

Let me be really clear here: my butler does not announce anyone else in the room. This is *never* how I see the other people around me, as only being worth my time if they are impressive and well-connected enough. In fact, in any social situation, you'll almost always find me off to the side, hanging out with the wallflowers and the introverts. These are also my *people*. But the truth is, we often think things about ourselves that we would never think about others.

Sometimes my butler doesn't show up to work.

And then I'm left feeling like it's *my* job to let people know they aren't wasting their time with me. I'll be in the middle of a conversation with some new person who hasn't been anything but kind to me, and I'll feel it start bubbling up inside me like acid reflux. First in my esophagus—a burning, bitter feeling in the center of my chest. And then in the back of my throat—the sour taste of insecurity, like orange juice meets battery acid meets three-day-old milk in a glass. I'll do my best to swallow it back. To chew up the not-so-humble brags and spit them out before anyone's the wiser.

But despite my best efforts, they inevitably come word-vomiting out.

First I'll have to mention Yale, but how I didn't become a lawyer. Next maybe it will be something about all the places in the world we've photographed. Or the courses that we teach and how successful that has been. The places that I speak. And did I mention I'm a writer now? Then I'll tell you about that girl in the trailer, but only so you can see just how far I've come since then. And how I'm definitely not her anymore.

Are you impressed yet, are you impressed yet, are you impressed yet?
Am I enough yet?
Am I somebody worth loving yet?

When I tell Kim all this, she asks me, "What is the *truth*?"

And we proceed to get into a *heated* debate about worth, and talents, and *to whom much is given, much is expected,* and where our true identity comes from. It's maybe the closest thing to a real fight we've ever had.

I tell her that for people like me, achieving is not a choice. Achieving is like our oxygen.

Perfectionism is the penance we pay for taking up space in any room.

We don't choose to achieve, and we don't do it to feel better than anyone else. We do it because somewhere, somehow, a switch got flipped in us. Something broke inside. On a very profound level. And we're not going back. Shattered into a million pieces. Like a mirror when we weren't ready to deal with the reflection. And every day we're out there checking things off a list, that's us trying to put ourselves back together again. Shard by jagged shard.

"Listen, I run toward success because that's just me trying to outrun failure." I tell her this with a detached dryness in my voice that I don't even recognize.

"I started running the day I left that trailer, and I haven't stopped."

At this I tilt my head back and stare up at the ceiling. My life playing out in warped scenes on the rippled plaster.

If I were making a joke here, I'd tell you that my achieving looked just like Forrest Gump when they hand him the football and tell him to "Run, Forrest, run!" Except no one ever tells him when it's safe to stop. So he just plows right through the end zone and keeps on running. *Victory after victory.*

But it's not like that.

My running is a girl in a red cape, barefoot and muddy, escaping her way out of the deep, dark woods. Branches clawing at her skin, tearing at her clothes, leaving chunks and pieces of her behind like breadcrumbs. Something chasing, always chasing, close behind and closing in fast. The big bad wolf *ripping* at her heels.

She runs because if she stops, she knows it just might kill her.

I am the girl in the red cape.

But when I turn to look back over my shoulder, breathless and wild eyed, I see it.

I am also the wolf.

And that voice in my head telling me to run and not stop running—that it will *never* be safe for me to stop?

That voice is my own.

I tell Kim this, and she sighs hard and then takes a blue marker to a piece of poster board on my white kitchen island. She writes my name big across the top, then lists out every big goal I have for the year ahead.

"So. Even if *none* of these things happen, not a single one comes true, what still remains?" She taps hard on my name. "Who is *Mary* without any of these goals?"

I know what she wants, what she's going for. I know I am supposed to say something about being a child of God, still loved and inherently valued by my Creator.

But instead, I scare even myself with how fast and loud the word "NOTHING" comes racing out of my mouth.

We stare wide-eyed at each other for a long minute, and then we nervously laugh. We have to laugh or we will cry.

My life up until that point has been spent running.

And no one ever told me it was safe to stop.

Achieving has been my oxygen.

But I can tell you right now, *it's no way to breathe.*

"SHE'S THE MOST put-together person in the room."

That's the lie we tell ourselves about who we have to be in order to earn a spot in any of the places we walk into. Whether it's the clothes we wear or the house we own or the pieces of us we so freely give away by saying yes when we really want to say no, we are all about the appearance of polished. The luster of confident and capable. Shiny on the outside.

Here's why: it is so much easier to be admired for the pretend version of us than it is to be truly loved up close for the hard, messy, broken person we might actually be.

Shiny is a stiff-arm. A Heisman pose. It's a way to keep people at arm's length. Far enough away where it doesn't feel like all these scars are on full display, still burning from the memory of the wounds that cut so deep in the first place. So no one can see, *up close and personal,* the grit we still have under our fingernails from the last time we dug ourselves knee-deep out of the mud.

Shiny is safe. Shiny is certain.

Shiny is also a cop-out.

We get really good at putting on all sorts of capes and cover-ups for the world. When I think about the masks we wear, here I can't help but picture Mrs. Doubtfire rising from the refrigerator in her meringue. *Hellllooooo.*

We layer on "more" like sweet buttercream frosting, don't we? We take the parts of us that are soft and delicate, in danger of crumbling, and then we heap on more. We tell ourselves we have to do more and *be* more if we are ever going to be worthy. If the world is ever going to love us.

And . . . it's exhausting.

And I think we should all agree to stop doing it—to ourselves and to one another.

Because what if I told you that all along, the soft, vulnerable, delicate, partially crumbling center that makes up the core of you is what people are really trying to get to anyway. That in this world where no one slows down long enough to really talk to one another, more than anything we just want to see the real you. The one that's hidden behind all those layers of what you think you should be.

The buttercream just gets in the way, and that's why most of us can really only take it in very small doses anyway.

It's just far too sweet to be real.

We go out in the world wearing the armor of the well-adjusted, the sword and shield of the over-achieved, the cape that covers all manner of our most secret identities. Brick by brick we build a facade that we think is everything the world wants to see.

But then, when we step back to admire our work, we realize we haven't built a monument to how far we've come but a wall that now stands between us and other people. These capes and masks we wear are not just barriers that keep everyone else out. They are also a prison of perfection that keeps us walled in.

And we're suffocating.

But here's the thing. The true connection we crave most happens face-to-face. It happens when the mask comes off. When the walls come down. When we finally take off the cape and say, "It turns out I can't leap tall buildings after all. Will you still love me anyway?"

Honestly, when I really try to imagine talking to God, that's how I see Him. He sits crisscross on the floor across from me, way too close for comfort at first. Close enough to play the hand-slap game if He wanted to, our knees almost touching. He stares into my face so long and so hard that I know He could see every flaw if He chose to, every line before it is even formed. I refuse to make eye contact. Every hard, messy part of me is there on full display, and there's no point in trying to hide it. He knows it all.

I hang my head low, the weight of the shame and disappointment so heavy that my heart can hardly *bare* it. But instead of slapping my hands away, He gently counts every hair on my head. He lifts my face to the light of His own. I feel the warmth wash over me at once of being truly known and truly loved. He isn't going anywhere. He isn't walking out. He won't leave because somehow I wasn't enough of something to get Him to stay.

He holds my hands in His, and I cry hard, bitter tears for a lifetime of things I haven't yet allowed myself to grieve. I fall to tiny broken pieces in front of the Creator of the universe, every atom spinning in the orbit of His presence. And He just leans in closer. Quiet. Listening for the words I need to say. When I've told Him everything, cried for every hurt and every fear and every other way I've tried and failed to find belonging, He just puts a cool, comforting hand on my forehead and at once the pain begins to subside.

"That's okay," He tells me. "You just forgot who you were there for a little while. *And it's safe now for you to rest.*"

grace is a root word

GOLDIE LOVED A VERSION of me that didn't exist.

That's how it always felt anyway. When she looked at me, she saw someone much better than me. Better than I actually was.

In her gray-blue eyes I was sweeter, smarter, kinder, more thoughtful, and better behaved than any version of me that I had ever known. It was like she had on some sort of rose-colored spy glasses that she'd gotten out of a cereal box. Lucky Charms, probably. Or maybe Cap'n Crunch. The Cap'n always had something going on.

Only instead of decoding top-secret documents or making things look three-dimensional in that fuzzy, couldn't-possibly-be-real sort of way, those glasses filtered out everything about me that was selfish and prideful, envious and competitive, self-indulgent and lazy. Till all that remained was the good stuff.

Good stuff that I was pretty sure wasn't even there to begin with.

The way she described me sometimes, when we were out in public and she'd be introducing me to someone, I'd have to look around to see who she was talking about. When Goldie looked at me, she saw no wrong.

And honestly, it made me *really* uncomfortable.

Grace is a lot like that for me.

I think one reason it's been so hard for me to let grace get down and really take root in my heart is because it feels like God is looking at me through those rose-colored spy glasses. Loving a version of me that couldn't possibly exist.

"You don't know just how selfish I can be, God," I want to say to Him. "You don't know just how much pride I indulged in today. And let me tell You, it was a banner month for envy."

It's like I want to look out for God. Make sure He doesn't feel like He's been duped. It's like I am a car He's just paid the ultimate price to drive off the lot, and I want to make sure He knows that there's a lemon law. *You can return me if I'm not what You thought I'd be, Lord.*

When I get right down to it, here's what I think it is: I am uncomfortable getting something I can't possibly ever repay—for *free*.

Dad's lesson from Grandpa Bill echoes a haunting refrain in my mind: *"Boy, you don't take anything but what you can pay for."*

Every cellular mitochondrion of my being thrums out this one truth that I have been raised on since birth: you *work* for everything you get. It is *supposed* to be hard. If it isn't hard, you probably didn't earn it. You probably don't deserve it.

And then I turn around and here's eternity being offered to me for free.

Here's God looking at me and seeing no wrong. Introducing me as His child in a way that makes me look around to see who He's talking about. On His lips, a laundry list of good things about this version of me He now sees.

Blessed. Chosen. Adopted. Loved.

And I'm just supposed to be okay with that?

When God looks at me through the eyes of grace, He sees no wrong. He sees someone much better than me. Better than I actually am.

And honestly, it makes me uncomfortable.

Which is why I've spent way too much of my life acting like grace is far too fuzzy to be real.

A prize in someone else's cereal box.

A gift I couldn't possibly deserve, so I believe it's not for me.

THERE'S A PHOTO of Mom and me from when I was just a baby.

Donaldson's grocery store, down in the middle of Richwood, used to bring in a photographer once or twice a year. They would set up in the stockroom—backgrounds of nature scenes hiding shelves of Dr Pepper and detergent, a faux-wood split-rail fence to lean against, a box to sit on covered in a tarp of green Astroturf meant to look like real grass. And you could get your photo taken in front of all this for a mere twenty dollars.

In the photo, I'm at that doughy stage of baby where I can hardly hold my head up, probably due to the four extra chins I was carrying at the time. And Mom sits there—so beautiful in a high-collared shirt with a ribbon tied in a bow, her short dark hair feathered away from her face—and gently holds my head up with a well-placed pointer finger under my many, *many* chins. It's a very sweet moment.

But if you look just a little closer, there's something more.

Goldie was the first one to point it out to me. There, clasped tightly in her other four fingers forming a fist, is a folded-up twenty dollar bill. Goldie said Mom probably saved up for weeks to have enough money to get that picture made, and she was so worried about losing it that she wouldn't let it out of her sight. Not even for the picture.

I think a lot of times we have these moments we remember in our own minds of what it looked like growing up. But if we'll look just a little closer, there's a picture within the picture. A story behind the story. There's always something more.

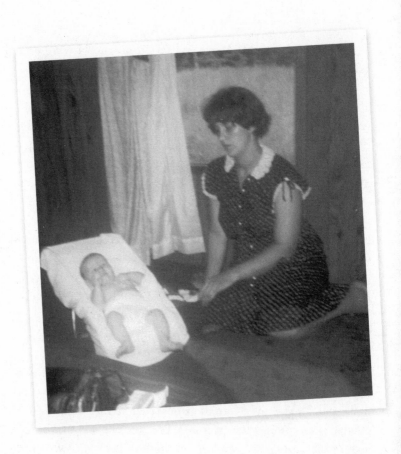

For a lot of years after Mom left to go work on the road for Ames, I acted as if she had packed up every part of me that had ever been like her and took it in the car with her when she drove away. Like some sort of redacted DNA. A black Sharpie mark through everything that reminded me of her. In every way, I became my father's daughter. I attributed every good thing in me to him. It was as though Mom was a mist, a memory in front of a watercolor backdrop. Scattered pictures of the way we were.

But the grown-up truth is, I'm a lot like her.

Sometimes I'll pass a mirror in the hallway, and for a fleeting second I'll catch her reflection where mine should be. Or I'll say something and swear I hear her voice instead. I'm stubborn like she is. I get my competitive streak from her. Occasionally I'll get mad and stomp out of the room, just like she always did.

But I also have a good, kind heart like she does. I see the best in people, and I know how to push them to bring it out. I am a natural-born leader, and I call people up to what they are capable of because I watched her do that for years. I'm funny in a really quirky way. I quote movies in a fluent way. I love fiercely. I give freely. I would save every last animal if it were possible. And I am driven to build a better life for my family than what I had growing up.

And when I see those things in me, I see *her*.

For years I told myself a story about a mom who left. About a mom who *wanted* to be gone.

But if you look a little closer, there's always something more.

LONG AFTER I WAS THE GIRL IN THE TRAILER, I ask Mom about her leaving.

She starts with the practicalities. Her job had the health insurance, her job paid the bills at a time when the logging business wasn't able to, her job made it possible for me to have things she never did. Toys. Activities. Class trips. Running water.

It's eye-opening just how practical it was. But I push her.

"Even if that part is true about the bills, wasn't part of the reason you left *also* that you wanted something that was *just* yours? Beyond just being my mom or Dad's wife."

She hesitates. We both know there's truth in that.

"Yeah, I guess in some ways that was part of it."

I wait, letting these words that have been hanging over both our heads for a lifetime finally land and take root. She goes on.

"You know, I always knew I wanted to go out and build a good life. Ever since I was little, I was determined to go do it. I guess I thought that's what I was doing."

"I get that," I say. "I know that feeling. Believe it or not, that makes sense to me."

And I mean it. I really do.

I know firsthand how powerful that drive is to go build a better life. How it gets into your red blood cells and won't let go. How it courses through your veins and brings little hits of oxygen to your brain with every microstep closer you get to that life you dream of. How it beats out an urgency in your heart. An internal atomic clock screaming at you that you're running out of time to change everything.

I'm not saying that I would have made the same decisions. I'm just saying I know what a siren song that good life can be.

"I can tell you now though," she continues, "it's been one of the biggest regrets of my life, leaving you."

At this she breaks down. And I quietly listen to her cry on the other end of the line.

There is truth in tears.

"I thought I was leaving to help my family, but it turns out I ended up *losing* my family in the process."

She cries more. I take a deep breath and exhale. A flood of oxygen fills my mind and finally I can breathe again.

"There's still time," I tell her. "I'm still here and you're still here."

There's still time for you and me.

We're both still here.

And we're both *still* family.

GRACE is a root word.

Not too long ago, Kim sent me this sermon to listen to. The preacher was talking about how God doesn't just want us to be messengers of grace but an *embodiment* of it. How He doesn't want us to just walk around talking intellectually about the idea—hiding behind our elbow patches and beautiful minds, giving formulaic lip service to what it means to cover all manner of wrongs—but to actually have grace be something that consumes us, changes us, transforms us from the inside out. An internal reckoning that transcends all manner of form or logic.

Grace is trying to *do* something in us.

Kim told me she sent me that sermon because it made a strong case for why relationship and reconciliation are always worth the fight.

But I think she also secretly sent it because she knew that my words would never have the kind of meaning I wanted them to until grace got deep down into my heart.

In school, I always loved geometry. I was *good* at geometry.

With all of its theorems and proofs, this was a language I understood. After all, a theorem, by definition, is a statement that can be proven. And a proof is just an argument that begins with what you know, proceeds through a series of logical deductions, and ends with the very thing you're trying to prove.

I'm *good* at ending things with what I'm trying to prove.

Even geometry itself, when you break it down to its roots, just means a measurement of the earth. *The logical study of the things of this world that can be proven beyond a shadow of a doubt.*

Geometry I get. Grace is sometimes a different story.

I've been good at talking about it logically. I've been known to set out the proof for why it matters. But until I let grace dig down deep into every chamber of my heart, until I anchored myself to letting love rule where logic always had, those words were just a theory.

Grace has the power to transform. It has the power to heal wounds so deep you thought they would never close over again.

But it only works, you'll only see the *proof*, if you are willing to let it take root.

I HAD THIS DREAM ONCE where I was standing in front of the trailer I grew up in.

Only it wasn't found where it usually came to rest on the top of our mountain. Instead, it stood alone in a great, vast, frozen land. As far as the eye could see, there was just ice and snow and emptiness. And in the middle, like an oasis, like a shelter in the storm, stood that brown single-wide trailer. The wind was whipping up a sandstorm of snow, and it hammered out a high lonesome sound as it pelted against the side of the aluminum.

An off-beat, driving rhythm calling me home.

At once, the scene shifted and I was inside, standing in my parents' old bedroom. Not a single thing had changed. Stacks of sweaters and a favorite gold necklace rested on one side of their dresser. On the other side, the contents of my father's pockets, which he emptied out every night: a two-handful mix of coins and bolts, thin metal washers, and thick chunks of mud. An artifact of excavation into how he spent his days.

As I stood there, the frozen ground began to shift and give way beneath me. The trailer started rocking from side to side, a marooned ship shaking loose to finally sail the freezing North Atlantic seas. With every rolling pitch, the trailer dipped below the freezing level, and the unforgiving water came rushing in, its icy fingers grabbing at my legs.

In a panic, afraid of losing it all, I found a garbage bag and began to fill it with things. Ratty stuffed animals and musty old clothes. My hands couldn't move fast enough to take it all with me. It was just then I heard a voice telling me that there was still time for me. That it wasn't too late.

But I first had to be willing to lay that junk down. This baggage I had been trying so hard to hold on to. These scraps of my life that no longer stood for what I thought they had. This supposed evidence of something always lacking, a scarcity mindset that now no longer served.

I listened for a moment longer to the snow battling against the windows, picking out the strung chords of a melody I was just beginning to recognize. It was a rhapsody and a reveille of a wake-up call that came to me once in a dream. It told me there is freedom in laying down these heavy things we were never meant to carry. Deliverance from the things that try so hard to drown.

In the final moments of a reverie, the rushing roar of icy water whispered to me.

Take every storm this world hits you with and turn it into a song.

the broken was
part of the plan all along

THERE IS THIS FAIRLY FAMOUS PROVERB that says, "Just when the caterpillar thought the world was ending, it became a butterfly."

I know that's meant to be inspiring. But every time I see that written somewhere, all I can think is, *I bet it hurts the caterpillar.*

I once gave a talk on this at a conference.

When I got to this part, I conjured scenes right out of *X-Men* about what it would look like to grow wings out of the back of your own body. Feathers protruding through raw, broken, bleeding skin. Clawing at the surface of these shedding outer layers that no longer seem to fit as this new version of yourself tries so hard to break through. A literal stabbing of your own back just to fulfill your natural propensity to fly.

It wasn't pretty.

And then there were the other people in the movie. The ones who tell you to hide your newly sprouted wings because they make you look like a freak. Well-meaning friends and family who tell you to cover up and blend in and go on being normal. Pretend that nothing has changed so that you don't make anyone uncomfortable with your newfound wingspan. Whatever you do, don't you dare defy gravity.

I bet it hurts the butterfly too.

After my talk was over, the sound guy, Mike, came up to help me out of the lavalier microphone setup.

"You know, it's funny. I was just reading an article about caterpillars and what happens to them in the process. They don't actually grow wings out of their back at all."

He had the sort of genuine, kind, hazel-green eyes that made that word "actually" not feel like an attack.

Great. There goes my analogy.

"What actually happens to them, is that first they disintegrate entirely. If you cut open a cocoon or chrysalis, that's all you would find. Caterpillar soup. But then out of that, they grow into an entirely new thing. This time, one with wings."

Mike later sent me a link to the article, and he was right. And I did a little more research too. It turns out that when the caterpillar is dying to be reborn, a tiny shroud forms over its broken body inside its tomb. A mourning of what was lost before the thrill of hope takes flight. A dying of self to become a new thing. A metamorphosis out of the messiest times of our lives.

It turns out, the broken was part of the plan all along.

I'VE BEEN THINKING a lot about transformation lately.

This becoming something new. The somebody we were always meant to be.

And here's what I've come up with. It's groundbreaking. Are you ready?

I think transformation hurts.

There's a reason the Bible talks about gold getting refined in the fire and clay only taking shape under the pressure of the potter's hands. *No pain, no gain,* so to speak.

But it's not just that.

Sometimes it can feel like our own transformation hurts the people around us too.

When I get right down to it, I think one reason it has at times been so hard for me to become the Girl After the Trailer is that this becoming someone new can also feel, at the very same time, like a betrayal of who you once were. Of the people and the places that raised you.

There's a phrase I once heard a second cousin of mine use: "She's acting higher than her raising."

It wasn't said about me, but it felt like a warning. An admonishment in advance.

It also felt like there was some implied ceiling each one of us is born with, and that to break through that is to risk the whole house falling down. Or at the very least, to spit in the faces of the ones who dug out and built the foundation in the first place.

How do you leave without saying there was nothing worth staying for?

How do you try for more without saying there was always something lacking?

How do you try to change things without saying they were irreparably broken to begin with?

Can you have it both ways? Can you somehow be both fiercely proud of where you come from and also fiercely determined to build something new?

I believe you can.

I believe you can look at your life—at everything you've become and everything you will be—and know without a doubt that you got there not *despite* these hard stories you bear but in so many ways *because* of them. And, at the very same time, I believe you can also determine to go out and be the break in those generational chains that will change your family tree moving forward. I believe you can go out and build a beautiful life with your own two hands, knowing full well that they might get muddy in the process. That you might get more than your fair share of scars along the way.

Build it anyway.

But build it knowing that your hands get to be muddy and scarred in the building of something beautiful, because someone else was first willing to get muddy and scarred in the building of *you*.

And that makes this life we're building now a redemption song, *never* a betrayal.

JR Bess wants to go to Hawaii.

I'm not sure when the joke started exactly. But for every Christmas memory I can conjure from the cobwebby corners of my tinsel-laced brain—here I want you to picture one of those rubber band balls made entirely out of 1980s silver icicle strands, the ones that used to get wrapped around the vacuum cleaner brush until it made that high pitched *squeeeeeeeal* and the whole room filled with that horrible burning smell—for every Christmas memory I can pull out of *there*, Dad got a joke gift about Hawaii.

It all started off as his fault, really. Every year, whenever anyone asked him what he might actually *want* for Christmas, rather than be bothered to come up with an answer, he always said the same thing.

"Oh, you know, just a first-class ticket to Hawaii. Same as nothing, that's a fact."

He said it with a joke in his voice, but his eyes looked so tired.

And so the jokes began. One year he got a plastic airplane to fly him first-class across the ocean. Another year he got a couple of fake flower leis that he could wear to Christmas dinner. There was the year he got Monopoly money so he could buy his ticket. And then there was the year he got Hawaiian Barbie. I'm pretty sure at least once a grass skirt was involved.

It was a joke. But each year that passed, it somehow became less funny. As if each year he was getting older but his dreams were just getting further away. The year he got Hawaiian Barbie, she came packaged up in a bigger box with his *real* gifts: thick socks, some flannel shirts, and a new pair of boots.

So he could get back out to work in the woods.

I was eight, maybe nine, but even I knew that was heartbreaking.

As the years passed, this running joke started to become a dream of my own. Every year for as long as I can remember, Dad asked me on Christmas morning if what I got him was a trip to Hawaii. And every year we just joked it off. *Hilarious.* It's the only thing he ever wanted. And probably never thought would come true. But somewhere inside the deepest part of my heart, I started counting down the days until that Christmas I could look him square in the eye and say yes.

This time he was right.

The Christmas it finally happened was nearly twenty years in the making. He opened a box with yet another plastic airplane in it and started to laugh it off. But when he turned that pretend plane over, on the bottom we had taped real tickets. *I wish you could have seen his face.*

Just a few weeks later, Justin, Dad, and I boarded a plane bound for Oahu.

Here's the first thing you need to know about that trip: Dad had never in his entire life been on a plane before. Not even a puddle jumper. So his first time ever on an airplane was an eleven-hour, nonstop flight to Honolulu.

We had to double-check his carry-ons for him before going through security, and I ended up pulling out two 32-ounce super-sized bottles of mouthwash and a *chainsaw* from his bag. Just kidding about the chainsaw, but the mouthwash part is true. I have never seen anyone pay such close attention during the safety announcements or look out the window more. For eleven hours straight, he announced every passing cloud to me and pointed out every mountain.

And when they passed the bags of peanuts around . . . he took two.

Our first night in Hawaii, we ate dinner under the stars. And Dad proceeded to get *real* introspective.

"Mary, y'know, I've had a good life, I can't complain. And I've loved logging, I really have. But it's just started to bother me a little, I guess, that when I'm gone there's nothing that I'll leave behind."

At this, he paused to take a sip of his "pog" juice—pineapple, orange, guava—of which he was now a connoisseur.

"You know, I cut things down for a living. And it's just bothering me that when I'm gone, there won't be anything that you or Justin or your kids someday can point to and say, 'Grandpa built that.'"

We all sit quietly at this for a minute, none of us quite sure what to say.

"I just think it's really something how you and Justin, just by the very nature of what you do with photography—just like ol' Matthew Brady and his Civil War photos—without ever doing anything else, you leave something behind that will live on long after you're gone."

He scratches at the white tablecloth with a dirty, cracked thumbnail. His eyes go liquid.

"I wish I had that."

HERE'S THE *SECOND* THING you need to know about that trip: Dad had never in his entire life gone swimming before either.

We packed the entire trip with activities. Helicopter rides, drives to the top of a volcano, French toast at Lulu's, and—his favorite—an entire day spent walking around Pearl Harbor, where I think he could have just spent every day and been happy, if I'm being honest.

On one of our last days in Hawaii, we booked a combination whale-watching and snorkeling boat trip. We figured that he would enjoy the first part with us and just hang out on the boat for the second part. But when we dropped anchor near a shallow cove, he went and sat on the edge of the boat and started putting on flippers and a mask.

He was going in.

Let me say again, *Dad had never in his entire life gone swimming before.* He didn't know how. In fact, up until that point, as far as I know, he had only ever been ankle-deep in the ocean. And now he was going *all* in.

When it came to getting in the water with our fins on, the crew gave us two choices: we could either sit down on the back platform and sort of scoot our way into the water . . . or we could go down their top-deck, two-story twisty slide and land with a splash.

Dad went down the twisty slide.

When he came back up, sputtering salt water through his snorkel and clinging for dear life to the foam boogie-board life preserver they had given him, he had the biggest smile on his face and gave me a thumbs-up. He stayed out there the whole time. He was the last one back on the boat.

Later I asked him, "So, Dad, what was up with going down the slide? Thought you didn't like the water."

He just laughed.

"Well, Mary, it's like this. When you spend fifty-some years of your life telling yourself that this one dream will never come true, that it's never gonna happen, and then it *does* . . ."

He searches for the words.

"Well, I guess it just makes you rethink everything else you've been telling yourself your whole life that you'll never get the chance to do."

A lifetime of doubts reduced to a single sentence.

NO ONE EVER TELLS YOU how hard it will be to watch your parents grow older.

When you're young, all you can think about is growing up and leaving home and making your own way in the world. And then one day you wake up and you've done it—you're grown, with a house and a family of your own. Though you're never really quite sure when it happened.

If you grew up without a lot, maybe you've spent the last few years making a nicer, warmer, prettier, happier, better-decorated home than you grew up in. Maybe it has wall art. An oversized Roman numeral clock or script lettering on faux-weathered wood. Maybe it has a nice kitchen island. White quartz—because you couldn't afford the marble—and gold pendant lights you once saved to your "kitchen dreaming" board. You once prayed for the *things* you have now. Maybe you've spent way too much on throw pillows. Just *so* many pillows.

No one ever tells you how much throw pillows will be a part of your adult life either.

But all along as you're growing up, your parents are growing older.

Looking back, in the weeks leading up to my leaving home for college, it was just one fight after another with Dad. The unstable breakdown of two complex molecules that had once been bound together. I had spent years trying to convince him to make a better existence with me. To somehow improve our station in life. If it couldn't be a real house, at least it could be a clean one. If we couldn't have more, at least we could take care of what we did have.

I remember the year I was thirteen, I went out in the snow by myself and hung strands of colored Christmas lights on our trailer. All along the aluminum and in crisscross fairy swirls all around the overgrown bushes in the front. A rainbow of fireflies twinkling in and out of existence, as if they were sparks burning up the winter night sky.

It was *almost* beautiful.

By the time my last bag was packed for college, I had also carefully stored away any misconceived notions I'd had about building this life together. This life I wanted I was going to have to go out and build on my own. But I knew that once I was gone, I didn't want that trailer following me, *haunting me*, while I hammered out this new existence.

This is where I need to get a little uncomfortable in my honesty with you. The truth is, back then I blamed that logging business for everything.

It was the needy sibling I'd never asked for, the one constantly getting Dad's attention. It was a problem child wrapped in a participation trophy, and he'd spent most of my life working all hours with hardly anything to show for it. He was constantly having to float money just to barely scrape by.

On one particularly bad fight, I stormed out of the trailer and slammed the door behind me. But not before turning back to say, "Let's get one thing straight. Once I'm gone, I'm gone. Don't you dare ever ask me for even one dollar to give that business. All it does is take."

It turns out it was a prophetic, if not very *pretty*, thing to say.

In the years to come, when the timber industry was taking hit after hit and he was spitting up blood so violently that it left its mark all over Goldie's green carpet, the bulldozer bill still needed to get paid or they told him they would come and repossess it. Apparently, that's what bulldozer companies do: roll all over people. So I paid it. And the month after that. And the month after that.

We told him to just let them *take* the dozer, that maybe it was finally time for him to retire. Told him we would help him do it. But he said he didn't know who he was if he wasn't logging. Said he felt like he would be letting his ancestors down if he quit now. That this was just the logger's way: showing up even when you don't feel like it, working through the pain, and doing exactly what you said you were going to do when you said you'd do it.

No one could question his determination. But still, I didn't like it.

Didn't like paying for something for the business—only to line the pockets of some big bulldozer company, not even something that would help Dad. Didn't like paying for something just so he could keep on working when I knew he wasn't able to. Didn't like it because what I feared more than anything was that logging would, faster than any cancer, finally be the death of him.

I didn't like it.

But I *loved* him.

And there isn't a hard-story person I know who hasn't had to come face-to-face with that tension. We hate the stubborn decisions but love the human.

And whether we pay the debt or don't pay the debt isn't really the point. It's not about the money. We know the money isn't really ours anyway. Really, this is about what we do with our *mercy*.

It's about leaning into love when it would be so easy to judge.

HERE'S THE THING.

You go into the world and you start to think the right couch or car or clothes will be your redemption. That a happy marriage, the 2.7 kids, a mortgage, an SUV, and the right school district with the gluten-free cupcakes will somehow set you free.

They don't. None of it changes your story. And you have to find a way to make peace with that or it will be the undoing of the rest of your life.

You get older, and you realize just how hard being an adult really is. You get older and you turn the same age your parents were when you were born, when you took your first steps, when you started kindergarten.

You get older, and you realize that all the time you were growing up . . . maybe they were just trying to grow up too. Two kids doing the best they could.

You get older and you mess up. A lot.

You realize just how often *you* need mercy too. And empathy floods like warm, golden light where once the stark winter landscape of bitterness used to reside. Like sparks of understanding lighting up the night sky, guiding your way back home.

For the first time ever, you see things from their perspective.

It's messy and hard, gritty and imperfect. That part you always knew. But now a new kaleidoscope of color glows in the darkness, reflecting scenes of your life on a white linen sheet of undisturbed snow. A string of grace, shedding light on a different part of the story. One of love and sacrifice and always doing the best they could. Of sometimes coming up short, just like you have, but never for lack of trying. And *never* for lack of love.

. Once you see it, you can't look away. It's hypnotic. It's humbling. It's haunting.

It's almost . . . *beautiful.*

at last freedom takes root
and comes home

AT A CERTAIN POINT, you stop running.

Breathless and at last exhausted, you double over at the pain of a lifetime spent proving. You've run so hard for so long. You've gone *so* far out into the world, only to keep finding yourself back at the beginning. You have spent a lifetime starting over, breaking loose to run free only to be taken captive again and again. This one truth always dragging, always clawing at your heels like the heavy chains you never asked to bear: no matter how hard you run, you can't outrun *you*.

So you crawl there for a while, panting through the pain, and then you curl up in surrender and rest your face on the cool, hard ground. Death to this old life you once knew. A mourning of what was lost before the thrill of hope takes flight. A dying of self to become a new thing—this time one with both roots and wings.

"God, set me free of *me.*"

Your fingers find the dirt beneath you, and they dig in. You feel the earth at once soften and shake loose to welcome you, a new way in the wilderness taking root. A wild thing. *Untamed.* This vine that now carries you is no shackle. This vine is color and freedom and fire and dirt. You feel a new kind of strength coursing through you now. There is *power* now, and you rise.

RISE.

You turn your face to the light and you welcome the fire. For even in the season of drought, these leaves will stay green. You *know* what it is you're anchored to.

These scars and these wounds, these raw nerve endings still smoldering from the burn—you no longer hide them. Instead, you stretch out your limbs and you turn every one of them to the sky. You let the air get to them. A cool, gentle breeze that finally quiets the sting. And the shame, like ashes, falls away at once. Mere dust on the wind.

From dirt it was born, and to dirt it shall return.

You stand there, at last on solid ground, no longer running. And your broken, scarred branches become a worship song. They are raised high now. Unhindered, unrestrained, unembarrassed. You reach childlike open hands toward heaven. And you just sway there, gently at peace. Standing tall among the giants. You can breathe again, you can rest.

At last, *freedom* takes root and comes home.

You know Who it is that holds you. Who has *always* held you.

You were born a wild thing.

And you are finally free.

Not too long ago, I heard a preacher say that often we are released in reverse.

And that really stuck with me. He said that sometimes in order to go forward in faith, we first have to look back and remember. I know he was talking about remembering how far God has brought us and that He will finish the good work He began in us. And that's so good and so true.

But I also think it applies to our memories themselves.

One of the greatest acts of freedom I ever experienced was allowing myself to feel empathy for the Girl In the Trailer. I had spent so long trying to get her to safety, telling her to run and not stop running, to run faster and not look back, to survive, to toughen up, to try harder, to get out, to deliver and overdeliver. To perform and perform and perform, until *I* told her it was safe for her to stop. I ran behind her and alongside her, sometimes in front of her and dragging her along when I had to. Always red-faced and screaming at her about how she had to try more and do more and *be* more if this world was ever going to love her.

And then one day, I finally said *enough*.

And I sat crisscross on the floor across from her, close enough that our knees could touch. Close enough where I could have kept playing the hand-slap game if I wanted to. But this time I chose not to. Instead, I stared into the face of a four-year-old me, and I gently counted every hair on her head. I lifted her face to mine and told her I was sorry for every hurt and every pain. For every time I ever told her she wasn't worthy of love just as she was. For everything I couldn't protect her from. I found myself falling to pieces in front of the littlest version of me, and she just placed a cool, comforting, tiny hand on the side of my face. Wiped the tears from my cheeks with her wide-open palms. And at once the pain began to subside, at peace at last with the strength that was always in our story.

"That's okay," she tells me. "I think it's safe now for *both* of us."

She's playing now. She's free. She dances around the room on a current of innocence and safety.

In between twirls, she holds my hand and whispers.

"And just so you know, I'm so *proud* of who we've become."

THE FIRST WAVE of freedom I felt was empathy for little Mary.

But the second wave that washed over me was when I found my way to that same empathy for the littlest versions of Dad and Mom too.

It was when I saw a version of them as little as I once was. Free. Unburdened. A moving picture playing out in slow motion, as if time and gravity themselves dared not interrupt that scene. I saw her freckled face and home-cut crooked bangs and skinned-up knees as she ran wild through the woods. Saw his ears, just a little too big for his body I guess, and the gap where all the trouble got in, smiling without a flash of worry or weary. For just a moment, then, I saw what they saw as little kids. What they lived through. What they set out to change and make different for *their* child one day.

Imperfect along the way, maybe. But the best heroes always are.

Kim told me not too long ago that leaning into freedom is a work in progress. It's fighting to take back reclaimed ground. That the freedom is already there, the ground has already been claimed for us, the land is already spacious. We just have to trust enough to have the courage to step out into it. She said each generation gets to build on the progress and healing that the generation before them made, and that generations to come will be better for the ground we take back now.

Most people hear a story of going from a single-wide trailer to Yale Law School, and they are interested in the upward explosion. Me, I got interested in the spark of change that came the generation before.

And going back—retelling my whole story from that perspective, a place where grace floods like warm, golden light—it changed *everything*.

Remembering what I had forgotten. Realizing what I never knew.

I was released in reverse.

And for me, it turns out, that was the only way *forward*.

IN THE YEARS BETWEEN Yale and Dad's hospital room, I went to work doing what I always said I would: building a life that was *different* from that trailer.

Justin and I bought a house in New Haven—a hundred-year-old fixer-upper by the sea—that we got in foreclosure when the real estate bubble burst, much like the pipe that had broken loose on the third floor and flooded all three levels. It had sat empty for six months after that in the heat of summer, until it was entirely eaten up with mold and the whole place smelled of mildew.

And when I walked in, it felt just like home.

We had the mold treated and then spent six more months stripping that house down to the studs. You've got to rid yourself of all that poison before you can build something new. When the contractors got down to the original construction—twelve-by-twelve solid-wood beams—they told us that it was because of what this house was made of that it was still standing. The integrity, the character, the legacy, the care with which it had been raised up, all made it possible that the bad stuff didn't truly get in.

"Don't just go for what's on the surface, Mary Ellen. You got to dig down to get to the good part." Goldie's words from a lifetime ago echoed in my head.

The first night Justin and I spent in the house, we ate dinner crisscross on the floor. Everything around us covered in tarps, a blue plastic bin and some candles between us for a table. Outside, a storm blew in over the water, the kind of earth-shaking furor that feels like it's got a hand pointed directly at you. The wind raged so hard that it rattled the windows and actually swayed the walls.

But it did not shake the foundation.

We held on to each other, he and I.

And despite the storms all around us, I was *safe, safe, safe.*

For going on ten years, we have been making that house a home. But there was no better day out of all of them than during that first month when they finished putting the new roof on. *Build walls around it, put a roof over it.* It was a real house now.

I was finally home.

THE PROJECTOR REEL was in fast-forward now, speeding up time.

A lifetime of scenes played out in the far-flung corners of a hospital room. They blurred and bled into one another, my past, present, and future all melting into one.

In the flickering, green, beeping darkness, the Girl In the Trailer and the Girl After the Trailer went and stood by my father's bedside. Knowing full well they both should have been willing to show up much sooner.

And tired of these once tightly stitched seams—the kind of hard-line barriers that now reveal holes when you hold them up to the light—those two separate lives of mine at last decided to unravel into one. These two separate versions of me I once thought I had to become in order to belong I now saw as common threads running parallel through the same story. Bound together in a patchwork pattern, like the quilted stars wrapped around the shoulders of a Fenwick Mountain sky.

The question still hung in the air.

As far as I knew, Dad hadn't prayed for anything or *anyone* a day in his life.

And I had no idea why he'd be starting now.

I asked him again when it was he started to pray.

"Oh, there were plenty of times when I was up there in the woods, and I'd say a little prayer that He'd get me out of there safely or help a tree come down without busting it up."

He's quiet for a minute.

"But I guess the first time I really talked to God and expected an answer was one night when you were about two years old," he said. "I opened the door in the trailer to your bedroom, and just a crack of light fell on your face. And I never knew I could love something so much. I prayed right there."

He doesn't have to think about the words. He's prayed them a thousand times since.

"God, I don't care what you do with my life, just do something with hers."

IN THE WEEKS AND MONTHS AHEAD, Dad would go on to have three surgeries and eventually be released from the hospital.

That same summer, the town of Richwood would be devastated by a once-in-a-thousand-years storm that washed over it in sheets and waves. A roaring boom that shook the mountains and flooded down Main Street. All the experts said the town would never come back. But there is an indomitable spirit that grows wild in the mountains where I come from. The same spirit that lives in that town. The same spirit that lives in Dad.

This love of doing what other people said could never be done.

It took a long time, but Dad went on to make a full recovery. And he started going to a little Baptist church near Richwood. The same little Baptist church where I had been saved when I was fifteen. The same church Mom started going to when she was that age. And the same little church where they had been married.

The past just has a way of repeating itself.

On a cold, snowy Sunday afternoon, a new preacher—a country pastor with a good heart—asked Dad if he'd like to give his life to God.

And he said yes.

Dad once told me that he felt like he wasn't leaving anything behind. That when he's gone there won't be anything to point to as proof that he was here.

But my life is the proof. This beautiful redemption song of a life I now sing.

There's a picture of my father's hands that I keep. Black and white. Muddy, scarred, and broken. It is a picture of sacrifice. There was a time growing up when I was embarrassed of those hands. Asked him to try to wash them clean once more or to hide those scars away. I'm not embarrassed anymore.

He looked at me through the eyes of unfailing love. He laid down his life so that I could be set free. His broken, battered body, offered as a sacrifice in my place.

And if that is not amazing grace, I don't know what is.

These are the hands of my Father.

These are the hands that built me.

epilogue

WE STOOD TOGETHER in the center of a carved-wood ball-room—an ornate white ceiling above us, a grand stone mansion all around us, sweeping views of salt water on the horizon—and for a moment, all of it disappeared. I was in a giant, ivory poof of a ballgown wedding dress, and Dad was in a tux that he couldn't wait to take off. An hour later, in fact—*hours* before the reception was over—he would change out of it and into a WVU T-shirt and hat that he had with him in his red pickup truck. But in this moment we were alone—surrounded by a multitude—two people from now different worlds orbiting each other on the dance floor as the first notes of Dolly Parton's "I Will Always Love You" filled the firmament of the room.

Earlier that day, he'd walked me down the aisle in a little white church, where Justin and I promised forever under an arbor made of wood that my dad cut and Justin's dad built. Josh came in to do a reading, and the Binghams Crew were thrilled to be part of a real American bridal party along with Aunt Lynn. Mom sat on the front row next to Dad, and the two of them cried together. Goldie, who was too sick by that point to make the trip, was never one to miss making an appearance. So our preacher made a big show of calling her on a cell phone at the beginning of the ceremony, and she listened to the whole thing with tears streaming down her face. Justin and I had people there from all walks of life who had made us who we are: our new photographer friends, his friends from back home, my friends from Yale, our families. And now all of them stood in a circle as I danced with my Dad. And there wasn't a dry eye in the room.

I held Dad's hand, and the scene went black-and-white in my mind, like it does when you're living in a memory you already know you never want to forget—not so much for what it looked like but what it *felt* like. And in the absence of color, I saw what really mattered. I saw in his giant hand on mine, a scar still stitched back together in the shape of an M. Saw the dirt still under his fingernails, no matter how much he had tried to scrub them clean that morning. Saw the cracks and calluses he had gotten from a lifetime spent building mine.

My mind drifted back in time to a girl with a mess of wild, curly brown hair—*untamed*—running freely now and without fear. She steps out from under a wooden overhang, a blanket of indigo above her, the skies her only limit, and she finally sees it. He would have given anything to hang those stars just for her.

I had always thought Dad ended up with the life he had because he didn't have any other choice.

But he *did* make a choice.

Everything he did was because he wanted me to turn out different from him.

But the truth is, I *am* like him.

And I owe my life to that.

This wild, wonderful, hard, gritty, broken-made-beautiful life. You may call it grace, you may call it sacrifice. But for me, the greatest of these is love. It is a song of redemption, a reconciliation with the roots that grew me, a melody born out of the muddiest parts of my story.

And it *always* started with dirt.

author note

THIS STORY IS ABOVE ALL a redemption song. Like most stories worth telling, it has hard parts, and I have done my best to make sure I'm not just relying on my own memory in telling them. Through hours of research, conversations with the people who appear in this book, digital evidence, photos, and journal entries, I have confirmed everything that could be, remembered what was forgotten, and learned things I never knew. There is a common writing adage that drafts of a book should go from true, to truer, to truest. This final draft is the truest version of my story that I have ever known, in large part because the people in these pages were willing to talk about both the beautiful . . . and the broken. For that, I am forever grateful.

Most names and identifying characteristics of the characters in this book have not been changed. However, in a very few cases we did change or omit names, characteristics, or defining details in order to preserve anonymity and to protect the innocent or the guilty, as the case may be. Particular events may have been combined or reordered to maintain the arc of the book, but only when that had no impact on the truth or substance of the story.

There is a part of this story where I talk about Dad making the decision to become a logger and not a coal miner, but I want to be clear that I have so much respect for both. They are both such hard, thankless, incredibly dangerous jobs where those men put their lives on the line to feed their families. For so long, both have been the backbone of my home state, and I am proud to have a long line of both loggers and coal miners running through my family tree.

Finally, that *is* the actual trailer I grew up in on the cover. Photo credit goes to Justin Marantz, from the first time I brought him home with me to West Virginia.

acknowledgments

I set out to write a book about the places you start. And in the process, I found myself somewhere brand-new. A spacious place, where empathy, grace, and redemption run free. In between the first and final drafts of this book, which could not have been more different, there was a gap—a great divide to cross—between where my heart had been for so long in unforgiveness . . . and a heart that is now wide open. I have taken to calling that bridge between the two—between these two different versions of a book and these two different versions of me—"But God." I would still be drowning in a mire of my own junk as a first-draft person . . . but God. His grace changes everything. And that is why the first thanks I have to give is always to Him.

There is a reason why authors need several pages for the acknowledgments section, and that is because one person alone makes a Word document, but it takes a whole crew of people to make a *book*. And I just so happen to have the *best* crew anyone could ask for.

To Justin, you are the love of my life and my very best friend. Thank you for seeing a constellation of complicated and being willing to lean in and look closer to connect the dots. Thank you for being my soft place to land, the orange juice to my chocolate cake, my life unordinary. You read every single word, multiple times, and listened to I don't know how many drafts. Thank you for telling me it was going to work, thank you for bringing an endless supply of snacks, and thank you for reminding me to be nice to your wife when I couldn't see the way forward. Most of all, thank you for writing the pages of this beautiful life we get to lead together alongside me. And to Atticus and Goodspeed, thank you for being my comfort dogs and all the snuggles. "We were together, I forget the rest."

To Kim, five years ago we sat at a table with popcorn between us and I told you that I wanted to write a book. And there hasn't been a day since then that you haven't been walking alongside me to see this book come to life. From reading multiple drafts to daily check-ins, you have pushed me to fight for something better than draft one, to believe that grace and reconciliation are always worth the fight. Thank you for whiteboarding it all out so I could finally see it: these two parts—The Girl Before and The Girl After—were always stitched together by a turning of the page called "But God." I'll never be able to unsee it now. Thank you for helping me silence the wolf. Thank you for helping me take back reclaimed ground. Thank you for loving CCB as much as I do!

To Kelsey, from the first moment we met I knew I would be the luckiest to get to have you as my editor. What I found out quickly, though, is that I'm really the luckiest because I also now get to call you a best friend for life. Thank you for seeing something in this book from the very beginning and fighting so hard for it. Thank you for pushing me to tell it my way and not be like anyone else. Thank you for reminding me to trust and serve the readers, to give and not hold back. And thank you for knowing when it was enough. Thank you for every encouraging note, for believing me when I said I knew it could be better, and especially . . . for the cupcakes! Just so you know, you've spoiled me. I now shall expect them, henceforth and forevermore in perpetuity, every time I turn in a draft to you from here on out!

To the entire incredible team at Revell and Baker Publishing Group, you complete me! Jerry Maguire style. To Amy for your brilliant, thoughtful copyedits that sharpened my writing and added so much clarity throughout, thank you for caring about these words (and plays on words) as much as I do! To Patti for designing the most beautiful cover ever. Every day during draft two, I said, "I want to write the words that are worthy of that cover." To William and the design team for making the interior every bit as beautiful as the cover. To Andrea, Mark, and Jen for sharing your incredible wisdom and guidance—they were like gold to me. To Eileen, Wendy, and Melissa for getting these words out into the world and believing that stories change stories. You guys are not just my publisher, you feel like family. This is not my book, it's ours.

To Heather, Kerry, Devin Lee, and the absolutely rock-star team at Choice Publicity. You ladies believed in this book when it was just a someday dream, and I will never forget that. You are the best of the best at what you do, but you are even better friends. From that first day on a rooftop in Nashville, you have felt like a sisterhood to me. You have had my back from the highest highs to the lowest lows and everywhere in between. You are smart, savvy, and can rock a red lipstick like nobody's business. But most of all, you are women of grace and integrity. Any person lucky enough to have you in their corner has already won. Whatever else happens from here on out is just the icing on the cake.

To my amazing agents at DCJA/Illuminate Literary Agency. Rachel, thank you so much for listening to a podcast episode and sending the email that changed everything. I am forever thankful to you and Blair for coaching me through the beginning of the proposal process and continuing to cheer for *Dirt*. To Don Jacobson, you are a giant among men! What can I possibly say to capture everything you did for me as we were pitching this book? What a crazy, exciting ride that was! Every phone call, every strategy session, you not only were a brilliant advocate on my behalf, you were the trusted friend pointing me back to God every step of the way. You deserve all the champagne! To Marty Raz for being the contract expert extraordinaire and walking me through every step. And to the one and only Jenni Burke, my sounding board, my amazing friend, my comfort and strength through the whole book-making process, my font of all wisdom, I am SO excited for what the future holds and everywhere we go from here!

To Elizabeth Evans, my incredible producer of *The Mary Marantz Show*, you are a magical unicorn and a force of nature all unto yourself. I literally do not know how you do it, but you continue to amaze me daily. From the un-gettable guests to every brilliant way you have grown this show, you always say "let me see what I can do" . . . and then somehow manage to DO that very thing that *no one,* me included, thought was possible. God was showing off when he brought you into my life. I would still be spending five hours trying to record a thirty-minute episode if it weren't for you.

To our ride-or-die best buds, Erin and Peter, you have been there every step of the way. From the very first day we sent the proposal out, to those first calls, to the book party, to the cover, to the final draft rewrite, you have heard me verbally process it all. Words! SO many emotion words. And you didn't run away! Thank you for being the kind of friends who stay, who show up, and who keep showing up. It changes everything.

To (now Professor) Joshua Weishart, thank you for believing in me when I didn't believe in myself. Thank you for being that kind of friend, for writing the check, for mailing the letter, for your love and kindness. It changed my entire life and I'll never forget that. You'll always have a fan in me.

To our families. Thank you to Dad for untold sacrifices that were made, for prayers that were answered, and for cutting the trees that built my future. I am like you, and that has been the greatest gift. To Mom, for letting me inherit your strength and that stubborn streak in us that never gives up. Thank you for wanting better for your family. I am like you too, and that is also such a gift. Thank you to both of you for being willing to embrace the hard along with the beautiful in telling this story. Thank you to Goldie for always seeing the best in me, for the curlicue apples, for *I Love Lucy*, and for teaching me what it looks like to lean in with love. You were my best friend and I miss you every day. And thank you to my new family—Nancy, Dan, Derek, and Melinda—for raising the love of my life, making me a Marantz, and making me part of this beautiful legacy of happy marriages.

And finally, to the readers. To every one of us with a hard, beautiful story to tell. I want you to know that God says, "I see your messy and I'm not afraid of it. Your broken will not make Me turn away from you." Thank you for living these pages with me.

Mary Marantz grew up in a trailer in rural West Virginia. The first of her immediate family to go to college, she went on to earn a master's degree in moral philosophy and a law degree from Yale. After ditching six-figure-salary law firm offers in London and New York and starting a business with her husband, Justin, together they have built a successful online education platform for creative entrepreneurs. Mary is a popular writer and speaker whose work has recently been featured by *Business Insider*, MSN, *Bustle*, and *Brit+Co*. She is also the host of the highly ranked podcast *The Mary Marantz Show*. She and Justin live in an 1880s fixer-upper by the sea in New Haven, Connecticut, with their two very fluffy golden retrievers, Goodspeed and Atticus.

CONNECT WITH
MARY!

Helping world shakers own the
muddy parts of their stories

For speaking inquiries and to join the community, head to

MaryMarantz.com

  @marymarantz #thebookdirt

If you enjoyed reading *Dirt*, Mary's debut book, please
help others discover it by leaving a review online
wherever books are sold! And share your favorite quote
or image of the book on your social media account,
tagging @MaryMarantz and using hashtag #thebookdirt.